John Fielder
in Focus

Colorado Nature Photographer and Environmentalist

Steve Walsh

PHOTOGRAPHY BY
John Fielder

Above: John Fielder, Charlie Nuttelman, and Rick Wicker off-trail in the Colorado high country
Prior page: Fireweed, East Fork Crystal River, Maroon Bells-Snowmass Wilderness
Left: John Fielder, by Ryan Hanson, 4th grade

Contents

Foreword, John Fielder 1
Introduction, Steve Walsh 3
CHAPTER 1: The Early Years, 1950–1963 7
CHAPTER 2: Exciting Journeys, 1963–1964 15
CHAPTER 3: High School and College, 1965–1972 23
CHAPTER 4: Into the Real World, 1972–1981 33
CHAPTER 5: A New Career, 1981–2019 45
CHAPTER 6: John the Family Man 53
CHAPTER 7: John the Photographer 67
CHAPTER 8: John the Environmentalist 87
Epilogue 109
Reader Resources 111

Above: John's favorite sunrise, in aptly named Sunlight Basin, Weminuche Wilderness

Left: Winter sunrise through the aspen trees, Williams Fork Mountains, Summit County

Foreword

Yes, at least as of the writing of this foreword, I am alive. Unlike Steve Walsh's other biographies, this one is about someone who is still "kicking." This is a book about life's successes and failures, losses and rewards, joy and sadness. It is a celebration of life and death and how lucky we are to be sentient creatures with two arms and legs, and two (or one) of a lot of other things, on a planet, in a solar system, in a galaxy, in a universe, and probably in an infinite multi-verse. Every day I think about how fortunate I am to be experiencing life on Earth.

Thank you, Steve Walsh, for helping me share the past 69 years of my life with others, especially the young people for whom this book is written. I hope that my experiences can be useful to you young readers.

I hope that you, too, develop an appreciation for the miracle of four billion years of the evolution of life on Earth and that this book will motivate you to not just "see" it for yourselves, but smell it, taste it, touch it, and hear it by getting outdoors. If you do, you will be different than you would be otherwise. You will be stronger physically, enjoy better mental health, live longer, and get along better with your fellow human beings.

I love photography, but I love nature more. I have lived in the most beautiful place on Earth—Colorado—for most of my 69 years and 276 seasons. Colorado has everything but an ocean: plains, deserts, river canyons, and of course, mountains. Combine that diversity with four distinct seasons during which each of these provinces assumes a different personality, and the photographic possibilities are infinite. Though the bulk of my photography is about Colorado, I travel the world and come home after exploring a new place each time saying to myself: "that was amazing, but I think I like Colorado more!"

Opposite: Autumn aspen trees, San Juan National Forest

In case you were wondering, I have been just about everywhere in Colorado. I have driven and hiked throughout the Great Plains, including the Pawnee and Comanche National Grasslands. I have explored the most remote parts of all 28 Colorado mountain ranges, photographed all of the fourteen thousand-foot-high peaks, and been to most of the lakes in these places. I have rafted the best parts of Colorado's rivers and canyons, from the upper Colorado to the Yampa and Green rivers, from the Gunnison and Arkansas to the San Juan and Dolores Rivers in southwest Colorado. Yes, I have been fortunate to experience most of Colorado's 66 million acres!

I have been given wonderful friends, helpful career associates, generous mentors, talented partners in the world of environmental advocacy, loyal customers, appreciative fans, and a loving and supportive family. I could not have achieved my goals without each of these. Without family to come home to after long, exhausting, sometimes solitary journeys into wilderness, I would not be in the place that I am today. All of you motivate me to continue venturing beyond this place.

My dad set a fine example for me about giving back to one's community. In his case, it was a city and state. In my case, it is a state and planet. I have tried to return some of what I have gained from marketing my photographs back to the two things that have allowed me to make my living in the first place, you and nature. I am an environmentalist who realizes that if people are not healthy, happy, and prosperous, nature will not be protected.

To you, the younger people in Colorado, I look forward to working with you to keep your planet the kind of place you would like it to be. I hope that that includes protecting clean air and water, pristine wilderness landscapes, and enough habitat for the millions of other life forms with which we share Earth. The challenges are great, but together, I have no doubt that we will be successful. Please feel free to call on me for help whenever you wish.

—JOHN FIELDER, Summit County, Colorado

Introduction

As the station wagon drove along, everyone looked wide-eyed out the windows. The sights and sounds of evergreen trees, the flowing streams, colorful flowers, and huge mountains were captivating. Traveling were seven curious middle school age students and two energetic science teachers. The car kept driving up the winding mountain road. Over the last few days, they had driven 1,600 miles from Charlotte, North Carolina to Estes Park, Colorado.

The car pulled to a stop. After riding in a car for so long that day, everyone's joints were stiff while climbing out. They smelled the fresh pine-scented air and listened to the chirping birds. Long's Peak, 14,259 feet tall, soared in front of them. A 13-year-old, John Fielder, craned his neck to look at this lofty granite peak. He turned to his favorite

The Roaring Fork below Longs Peak, Rocky Mountain National Park

science teacher, Mrs. Eunice "Dolly" Hickman, and said, "This is beautiful. I want to live here someday." How true these words would turn out to be. The image and thoughts of that day stayed with John.

At the age of 16, he worked as a ranch hand near Westcliffe, Colorado. There, the lush valley was bounded by more 14,000-foot mountains. During later visits to Colorado, John was still impressed by this magnificent landscape. The vision of towering mountains, fast-flowing rivers, golden stands of aspen trees, lush pine forests, and snow-covered terrain stayed in his memory. Three days after graduating from college, John packed up his car with only one thing in mind. He drove straight out to Colorado to start his productive life.

This is a story about John's life and how his early interest in nature developed into a passion for the preservation of the environment. What sparked his interest in photography? How did he learn to take such stunning landscape photographs? When did John become interested in conservation? What part does he play in protecting the environment? John has fought fiercely for a long time to protect the Colorado landscape he loves. It is also a very personal story about learning life lessons from both failures and successes, overcoming family losses, and working to make the world a better place.

—STEVE WALSH

John Fielder
He is a rainbow shining off a lake
He is footprints in the moss.
He is fields with elk and deer in it.
He is columbines in a field
He is the tallest mountain
He is a glare shining off a lake
He is the sunrise shining behind the mountains.
He is color flowers in the hills.
He is a billy goat lying down in a field
~Max

John Fielder, by Max, 4th grade
Opposite: Bighorn sheep, Rawah Wilderness

CHAPTER 1

The Early Years
1950-1963 • (Birth-13)

John Fielder's father, John Thomas Fielder, Sr., grew up poor in Texas. He earned money picking cotton and watermelons. Life was busy with schoolwork, helping out at home, and outdoor activities. Then one day in 1941, Japan shocked the United States and the world. They suddenly attacked Pearl Harbor. In response, the United States declared war on Japan. World War II began for the United States.

John Sr. joined the United States Navy and was the captain of a C-47 transport plane. Brave crews flew hazardous missions over the Pacific Ocean from California to the Philippines. Can you imagine flying thousands of miles over dark water in stormy weather? High winds threw the planes around like confetti. How nerve-racking to be constantly on the lookout for attacks from Japanese airplanes! They transported munitions, that is,

John Sr. and Betsy, 1949

materials used in war, especially weapons and ammunition, food, and other equipment to the U.S. troops fighting against the Japanese Army. On the way back, the remains of American servicemen were brought home. After the war, John Sr. worked for the Navy Department in Washington, D.C.

John Sr. met John's mother at their workplace. After dating for a time, they got married. John's mother, Elizabeth Holland, "Betsy," grew up with two brothers in Washington, D.C. She was "very kind to others, independent … she enjoyed doing her own thing and was not too worried about what others thought of her," John said. John was born on August 2, 1950, in Washington, D.C. A year later, the Fielders moved to Rye, New York. John Sr. took a job in the department store business in New York City. He rode a train every day about 30 miles to work in Manhattan, a borough of New York City. John Sr. proved to be an excellent businessman. In 1956 he was offered a job running an entire store. With another child on the way, the family moved into a larger home in Greenwich, Connecticut.

John's second birthday, 1952

Family experiences shaped John's life. He was an only child for seven years. Being on his own helped John develop his independent personality. Then, brothers Bill and Jim came into the family. John now shared his parents' attention with two other siblings. Betsy cheerfully raised the children and participated in their school activities. She was comfortable letting John play outside for hours.

John liked where he lived. "Connecticut had bucolic (pleasant countryside) scenery, deciduous forests, and seemingly endless winding roads in the countryside," he said. "It was very much like the countryside that author Henry David Thoreau described in his writing. Like Thoreau, I found that nature was the perfect place for sensuous experiences." (Later, John discovered a book with impressive landscape photos and Thoreau sayings that impacted his life immensely.) During his childhood, John spent hours exploring the woods, climbing trees, and looking for creatures in the water. Besides these experiences, John also had fun in other ways.

Many exciting adventures awaited the Fielders in New York City. They liked going to baseball games. Huge crowds roared at games in the old Yankee Stadium. John especially enjoyed watching Yankee All-Star Mickey Mantle. He hit many home runs and made exciting plays in the field. During the holiday season, as they walked along the sidewalks, the children looked wide-eyed at thousands of bright lights and decorations. The Fielders browsed through the largest toy store in the world, FAO Schwartz. How exciting for the kids to see rows upon rows of colorful toys and packages! Visiting New York was a treat for the family. Then, a significant turning point happened in John's life.

"I'll never forget my first experience of riding my bike without the training wheels at age six. I felt freer than ever before. I sailed on that bike along country roads through the suburban forests of Connecticut. My senses were recording memories: sounds, sights, smells, and sensations of touch were being indelibly embedded in my mind. This memory has never gone away in 69 years. The joy of being on my own, exploring the world, the planet, that's where it all started." The freedom to experience nature by himself exhilarated John.

John (left) and his best friend Rocky played baseball and rode their bikes together in the countryside.

John's family lived on the outskirts of town near woods and fields. It was common for John to tell his mother goodbye and go explore outside for a few hours. He had many adventures alone outdoors. On the weekends and during the summer, he adventurously wandered in the woods and watched wildlife. "Can I climb that tree? Can I scramble over that high rock wall? What kind of creature can I catch today?" John asked himself.

Often, he went by himself, but he also liked going with his friends, too. He was curious about everything out there. John's connection with nature grew. His independence blossomed while spending so much time in the woods. Then, his father made a decision that added a new chapter to the family history.

John Sr. was offered a new job in Charlotte, North Carolina. Should he leave his present stable and high paying job? Was it best to uproot his family from a comfortable home? In the new job, he would work extra hours to make the business grow. His family would settle in an unfamiliar place. He thought about it and discussed it with Mrs. Fielder. John Sr. believed it was worth the risk to change jobs and move to a new place. This would improve his career and support his family well, so John Sr. took the new position. John was 10 years old when the family moved to Charlotte.

John's family grew to four children with the birth of his sister Holly. Betsy Fielder worked hard raising four active kids. "Mom was a nurturer," John recalled. "She generously took care of the kids so they could achieve what they wanted to accomplish. She lent help and advice when needed. However, she was opinionated and not timid. I probably inherited my rebelliousness from Mom." Betsy liked playing tennis and golf, maintained one of Charlotte's largest vegetable gardens, and was a great Southern cook.

According to John, his father was "...disciplined, very polite, somewhat formal, an active sportsman who played competitive tennis and golf. He was well-organized, a great planner, and a problem solver. I inherited my organizational skills, common sense, and business skills from my father." John Sr. raised money for Charlotte Country Day School, which all four kids attended. He was also in charge of the United Way in Charlotte. "He set a wonderful example of generously giving back to his community. This stayed with me all my life." John copied his father's example by one day giving his time, talents, and money

Chapter One: The Early Years 11

John Fielder, Sr.

generously to environmental and humanitarian organizations.

John's family lived on the outskirts of Charlotte. Life in the outdoors here was similar to Connecticut. Like before, he explored for hours alone and with friends in the fields and woods. He listened for the sounds of animals and birds, smelled the pines, examined ponds, touched the bark and leaves of the trees, picked up rocks, and tasted wild blackberries. The freedom of exploring was exhilarating. Not far from his house were clay soils that "percolated" buried American Indian arrowheads. When it rained, or the soil dried up, they rose to the surface of the ground. He traveled to the Blue Ridge Mountains with a friend and his dad to hunt for Appalachian Indian arrowheads and ax heads located where the tribes once lived. Here is where John started having his first conscious recollections of science, history, and nature. John thinks this was also the basis for his future artistic creativity: "After school was out, we had no schedules, only time on our hands and the need to decide what to do with it. To avoid boredom, we 'created' our own activities, alone or with friends. This freedom energized the thought processes."

For four summers, from ages 10 to 13, John attended Camp Sequoyah, a highly regarded outdoor boy's camp. It ran for five weeks in June and July and was nestled in the forested foothills of the Blue Ridge Mountains outside of Weaverville, North Carolina. It was the perfect place to help active and curious young boys develop an appreciation for nature. This was in a much larger setting than what was outside their back doors at home.

The camp provided tetherball, soccer, arts, crafts, riflery, and archery. The campers enjoyed field trips to Roan Mountain, Mount Mitchell, and Linville Gorge. Walking on the trails through a thick forest and jumping on rocks while crossing over streams was fun and exciting. Smelling the pine trees, listening to the birds twittering, touching the cold running water, and looking over the landscape from the top of a mountain was inspirational. Craggy Gardens was another favorite place to visit. It had colorful pink rhododendron flowers, tree-tunnel walking trails, and views of tree-covered rolling hills and mountains. John also learned how to avoid large timber rattlesnakes in the woods by watching closely for them. "Camp Sequoyah was my first hardcore nature outdoor experience, and I enjoyed it. This was also my first social experience living 24/7 with a lot of other boys and adults."

Camp staff taught local history, American Indian crafts, and lore of the Appalachian Mountains. Cherokee, Tuscarora, and Iroquois tribes lived here. The camp lake's temperature was a bone-chilling 48°. After getting used to the cold water, the campers enjoyed swimming and boating in it. John appreciated the scenery at the camp. He took pictures with a Brownie Hawkeye box camera which used black & white film. John looked down through the viewfinder on top and pushed a button to take the picture. The camera was a little smaller than a square tissue box. What a simple beginning to a later lifelong passion! In each of the cabins lived nine campers and a camp counselor. Pillow fights and pranks were not out of the ordinary. Campers helped

John with brother Bill being dropped off at Camp Sequoyah, 1960

Camp Sequoyah, 1960

take care of the cabin, and the counselors taught them how to get along with others. John's positive outdoor experiences at this age continued to inspire his lifelong fascination for nature.

In 1960, John started attending Charlotte Country Day School, which was founded in 1941. It included kindergarten through 12th grade. John's parents wanted their children to get a good education from a private school. Mothers and fathers of students participated in many school activities. The school had a strong curriculum in math, science, literature, the arts, and athletics. Teachers taught students to listen and learn from each other. The school had high academic expectations and encouraged students' creativity. John came up with many imaginative ideas in his artwork. He blossomed in this environment. Later, John had many important experiences outside the classroom.

Boys will be boys! It was easy to know when the 4th of July came around each summer. Colorful fireworks, bottle rockets blasting off, and many firecrackers popping reminded people of the holiday. More powerful firecrackers were illegal in North Carolina. John, ever the problem-solver, and his friends rode their bicycles nine miles to Pineville, South Carolina to buy them. They brought them home and joined in the fun. John and his friends exploded more than a few cherry bombs and M-80s, to the consternation of their mothers and fathers. "I loved learning," John said, "but I also enjoyed exploring personal boundaries!"

CHAPTER 2

Exciting Journeys
1963-1964 (Ages 13-14)

John went on adventurous field trips during his middle school years. He visited many unique places in the United States, Mexico, and Canada. A very extraordinary individual taught him inspiring life lessons. "One of the greatest single influences in my life was Mrs. Eunice 'Dolly' Hickman," John said. "She was a science teacher who was effective in the classroom, but exceptional for what she did in the summers." She drove students on five-week-long road trips every summer for 20 years. Mrs. Hickman used her own station wagon (like a minivan) towing a pop-up camper. Ten people squeezed into one car! She took seven students, her daughter to help manage the activities, and a fellow geologist teacher. Each day was planned out and brought a completely new experience. "She was a sparkplug, a good planner, focused on productivity, and skilled at bringing out the best from each individual," John remembered. She had a pleasant

The station wagon and the pop-up camper

Sandstone shapes, Roxborough State Park

personality and showed great patience with each person. She could be stern, but not unreasonable, as a disciplinarian. She accepted teenagers for their excitable and unpredictable ways. What a challenge it was keeping seven middle schoolers occupied and at peace with each other in the tight accommodations of the station wagon.

In 1963, on the first of these trips, the group drove thousands of miles and made many visits to interesting places. Together, they talked for hours, joked, ate, hiked, explored, and camped. They stopped in unique natural or historical areas. On special visits they dug for fossils and archeological artifacts. There was a valued place to sit in the car. "The coveted seat was in the 'way back,' which was a storage area. You could sit sideways by yourself and dream about what you wanted to dream about and have some downtime without other kids squeezed next to you," John said. Since this was before cell phones, a person either looked out the windows or closed their eyes to deal with the boredom of riding long distances. All of these activities and travels sparked John's sense of curiosity.

The 1963 route went from Charlotte through the southern states over miles of rolling hills and fields. Once, they stopped in a city park in Baton Rouge, Louisiana. During the day, John and his friend Philip talked to some girls there. Later, in the dark, John and Philip secretly rolled down a hill in their sleeping bags. Then they walked to an area near the public restrooms to hang out with the girls. Afterwards, the boys stealthily snuck back into camp, smiling at each other thinking they had fooled Mrs. Hickman. Soon after they woke up the next morning, they quickly found out that they weren't as smart as they thought! She threatened to fly them back to North Carolina if they pulled that stunt again. The boys got the message. After that, the drive continued through Louisiana and a long dry stretch across Texas.

Mrs. Hickman had a friend in Texas who owned a geode rock field. Geodes have a cavity inside that contain bright crystals. The group stopped here. It was exciting hunting for the round, rough looking rocks with a surprise in the middle. Rock hammers were used to break them open. John enjoyed "cracking open plain rocks and finding clusters of purple and white crystals inside." Then, they journeyed to Mexico City. "I remember not being able to see very far in the city. At 7,384 feet above sea level, the exhaust fumes from cars and buses were trapped within 'air inversions' among the buildings and streets. This happened long before mandatory air pollution controls were put in place for cars. It was like Denver in the 1970s."

The group then drove to Taxco, the silver capital of Mexico. Here they bartered for silver jewelry. They were

An important stop near Mexico City was at Teotihuacan, where the Temple of the Sun and the Temple of the Moon were located. It was also known as Mexico's "Pyramid City." Everyone piled out of the car and proceeded to climb the 248 steps to the top of the Sun Temple. An archeologist friend of Mrs. Hickman, who worked at the University of the Americas, gave them permission to dig there. They were even allowed to keep the relics they found. Strict laws prohibit this today. Excitedly, they dug in the soil and rocks and found ancient ceramic artifacts. Imagine finding archaeological items on a field trip! Carefully, they packed them away to take home. John treasured these 2,000-year-old pieces. They are prominently displayed in his home today.

Ceramic artifact from Temple of the Sun, Mexico

impressed by the ornate Santa Prisca Cathedral, interested in the whitewashed houses, and surprised by the cobblestone streets. After their visit, it was on to a new adventure.

The travelers then journeyed to the rocky, lava-covered Paricutin Volcano. Usually, volcanos were located in mountain ranges, but this one erupted in a farmer's field in 1943. Upon arrival, everyone climbed out of the car and gaped at the 1,391-foot-tall volcano far away. The plan was to climb to the top. What a task! They noticed the sky was filling with dark clouds. Their trip guides led them on "very skinny" horses across 13 rugged miles of volcanic ash fields to the volcano. A raging hailstorm arrived while they climbed the tall cinder volcanic cone. They were huffing and puffing as they scrambled up the rocks to the top. The boys got soaked and began to shiver. Then the group walked and slid back down to the bottom. They shook violently while riding

Taking the mules down to Phantom Ranch at the bottom of the Grand Canyon, August 1963

the horses back to the car. It seemed much farther than 13 miles away through the rain and hail. Upon entering the vehicle, they "jabbed their fingers" into the car heaters to defrost them. Their bodies were almost frozen and hypothermic. The cold boys changed quickly into dry clothes. Now, sitting in a warmed-up car, everyone felt relief. The travelers were definitely ready for warmer weather. They headed north to Arizona on the way home to North Carolina.

John loved the adventures during this trip. Camping out, exploring the ruins and rock field, and climbing the volcano were great experiences for the travelers. It was exciting to learn much about paleontology and archeology. But John also broke the rules when he and the other boy snuck away from camp. Was he going to be invited back for another trip next year? Mrs. Hickman thought it over the following year and decided to take him. This was a big relief to John, and he was impressed she gave him a second chance.

In the summer of 1964, the travelers were off on another long five-week road adventure. They drove 1,600 miles straight through the central United States across the rolling Great Plains. It seemed like endless miles going across the flat prairies. Then, after all the miles driven, the group looked farther west and saw jagged mountains in the distance. How exciting! After driving 100 more miles, they arrived at the steep foothills of the Rockies.

They started driving uphill on a winding forested road through rock formations, pointed peaks, and steep canyons. Then around a sharp corner, they came upon a scenic panorama. In front of them, Estes Park laid in a rugged valley surrounded by tall snowcapped mountains. What an inspiring sight. Mrs. Hickman drove cautiously down the steep and twisting road into the valley. "I'll never forget camping in Rocky Mountain National Park and seeing Longs Peak for the first time. At 14,259 feet tall, Longs dwarfed North Carolina's tallest mountain, Mount Mitchell," John said. John was fascinated by the lofty peaks, rugged granite summits, massive aspen groves, cold glacial streams, and alpine lakes. What a thrill to visit and camp in such a beautiful area! "That night around a campfire I told Mrs. Hickman that I would live in Colorado someday," he said. "Little did I know then how auspicious was my statement!" John would explore and photograph the entire 358 square miles of the park later in his life.

From there, they drove among mountainous areas and through forests and open prairies to Oregon. The group came upon a vast tree-covered escarpment. They went up a winding and heavily forested road to the top. It was the rim of a huge volcanic crater. They peeked over the edge and were stunned by the sight. Inside the crater was Crater Lake, the deepest, bluest lake in the United States. It was 1,949 feet deep. In the middle of the lake was Wizard Island with a 755-foot-tall volcanic cone. They drove down to the lake on another twisty road. A short boat trip took them through the crystal-clear water out to the island. Everyone scrambled on loose scree (small rocks) up to the top of the cone. Hands and feet slipped as they climbed. What a view from high above the water! The massive volcanic rim surrounded them. John slid back down upright on the loose scree and thought, "This must be like skiing, sliding down on feet." (Years later John would become an expert snow skier.)

From Oregon, the group traveled past mountain ranges and endless valleys to Glacier National Park in Montana. They saw rugged peaks, immense glaciers, and fast-running streams. They camped on the shore of Lake McDonald. The next day, a boat

With his friend the squirrel, Glacier National Park, August 1964

took them through the icy cold water to the base of Grinnell Glacier. The toe, or end of the glacier, was partially submerged in the water. They hopped aboard a snow vehicle with treads known as a snow-cat and motored up the steep ice and across the glacier. The vehicle drove near deep cracks in the ice with cold water flowing in them. When John visited the area 45 years later, he noted that "…due to global warming, the toe of the glacier had melted 8 miles farther up the mountain."

Next, the group drove long miles into British Columbia, Canada and over to Banff and Jasper National Parks in Alberta. More mammoth blue lakes, rocky crags, forested hills, and even taller mountains awaited them. They explored and camped there and used their rock hammers to break open fossils. Then, they began the long drive back to North Carolina.

These trips had a significant impact on John in many ways. "Those two summers were formative, for sure," he said. "We were studying science in its natural setting, exploring wild places, and camping out. We became comfortable being outdoors in sleeping bags under the stars by the age of fourteen." Mrs. Hickman planned these trips thoroughly. She sparked the students' curiosity in nature, geology, paleontology, and archeology. With ten people in a station wagon, this required, among other things, teaching the kids to pack only what they needed. John used these and other new skills extensively for the rest of his life. He saw many wondrous panoramic views on these journeys. An appreciation of nature penetrated deeper into his heart. He also continued to enjoy taking pictures and sharing them with family and friends. With these summers behind him, it was time for high school.

3
CHAPTER

High School and College
1965-1972 (Ages 15-21)

Charlotte Country Day School was also John's high school. He called it "a very disciplined private school where you did a lot of homework at night. School lasted until 3:00 and sports practice until 5:30. Then you went home, had dinner, and did homework until bedtime. The weekends were your free time." John learned from this well-organized schedule how to balance time between family, friends, and schoolwork. He also enjoyed other activities such as playing tennis, baseball, football, and basketball. Taller than average, John grew to be six feet three inches tall. He liked solving life's problems, and math intrigued him. John prospered in all these activities. His parents gave him a lot of freedom, support, and encouragement. At the same time, John admired his father's achievements and wanted to be successful like him.

Jumping center (#35) on the high school basketball team at Charlotte Country Day School, 1967

Foggy cottonwood trees, Highline Canal Trail, Greenwood Village

Mr. Tony Birch, the high school art teacher, enthusiastically taught students art appreciation and encouraged their creativity. "Mr. Birch was a mentor to all and had a low-key personality. He was a listener, a good teacher, and created incentives for artistic creativity. He was there when you needed him," John said. Mr. Birch knew his students well and elicited (drew out) their specific individual talents. He taught John not to be self-conscious about the quality of his work in clay and paints. How John felt personally about his work was more important than what others felt. He painted from 1966 to 1973. Later, all of this influenced John's photography.

John's 3-dimensional art influenced by the "pop" art era of the 1950s, 1968

Meanwhile, John's Uncle Fred became the head of the Colorado Fuel & Iron Company (CF&I Steel) in Pueblo, Colorado. Using iron ore, they manufactured railroad rails, steel pipes, and barbed wire. Its many steel products built the West in the 19th and 20th centuries. Central Colorado produced some of the iron ore they used. Hardy immigrant men and women from Europe mined coal in Crested Butte, Colorado. The rest of it came from New Mexico, Wyoming, and Mexico. CF&I also supplied coal for power plants.

Like Mrs. Hickman, Uncle Fred was another of John's mentors. He found John a job during the summer of his junior year in high school. "Hey, Tom, do you want to come to Colorado?" Uncle Fred asked. "I think I can get you a job." "Tom" was John's family nickname. Uncle Fred's acquaintance, Chet Haga, owned the Naja Ranch. It was nestled below the scenic Sangre de Cristo Mountains in the Wet Mountain Valley of Colorado, near the town of Westcliffe. This was west of the historic mining town of Silver Cliff. Nearby were Crestone Peak,

Crestone Needle, and Kit Carson Peak, all fourteeners (mountains higher than 14,000 feet above sea level).

This ranch raised white-faced Hereford cows and Quarter Horses. Chet bred these horses to be the fastest racers on a quarter-mile long track in nearby Pueblo. John worked the whole summer as a ranch hand. He woke up at 5:30 a.m., ate a big family breakfast, and labored until 7:00 p.m. six days a week. Sundays were his day off. Chores included fixing barbed wire fences, constructing a barn, driving tractors and bulldozers, bailing hay, and taking care of the cattle and horses. For the summer, Chet gave John his own horse named Blacky, who was three years old and a very fast racehorse.

Chet told John never to run this former racehorse in a straight line at full speed like at the racetrack. Chet wanted to change Blacky into to a "cutting" horse, which is trained to "cut," or separate, cows from the herd. Running this horse

A great place to gallop on a horse, the Naja Ranch, Wet Mountain Valley, July 1967

straight ahead would disrupt its intensive training. But John was a fan of sports car racing in North Carolina and loved the feeling of speed. He had an idea. Chet and his wife departed the ranch one weekend and left their son Mike and John in charge. John never forgot what happened next: "I saddled up the horse just to see how fast it could go and probably hit maximum Quarter Horse speed of 45 miles per hour at full gallop." Chet found out when he got home and wasn't happy at all. For not following his directions, Chet took away one of John's days off. John worked 14 straight days. He didn't run Blacky like that again.

John explored the Sangre de Cristo Mountains and took photos with a new "rangefinder" camera. He enjoyed sharing the pictures with family and friends when he got home. The joy of saying to others, "Can you believe what I saw and how beautiful it all is?" influenced his passion for sharing and selling his photography later in life. Spending time alone in the mountains continued to elevate John's curiosity and appreciation of nature. The next summer, John worked in his father's department store. He learned more details about the retail business, valuable experience which would help him in his photography career. Other formative things were building John's personality.

"In high school, I felt somewhat constrained," John recalled … "So many people—headmaster, teachers, sports coaches, mother and father—were guiding me through life. That's what they are supposed to do, and it was always in my best interest. On the other hand, I knew

Upper Brush Creek drainage, Sangre de Cristo Mountains, 2017. John developed a life-long passion for exploring the first place he ever photographed in Colorado, the Sangres.

that I enjoyed doing things on my own, making my own mistakes, and having my own successes. It was a learning process for sure, and not always productive. But it was a very good method to learn the best way to do things, that is, by trial and error. For me, college was the first opportunity in my life to be almost completely independent."

In 1968, John started attending prestigious Duke University. It is located in Durham, North Carolina, 143 miles from Charlotte. College was much different than high school. Students picked their own classes, made up their schedule, and did homework when they wanted. John took courses in accounting and management science. John's goal was to succeed in business with an accounting background. He also enjoyed learning about managing businesses. After his first year, John joined a fraternity, a men's society. There were 54 other members, "…a large mix of different kinds of people," he recounted. John made many friends. While working hard at a demanding institution they had a lot of fun by pulling amusing pranks on each other. As a newcomer in the fraternity, he was once kidnapped by his "brothers" (fraternity members). He was driven 15 miles outside of town at midnight and locked in a Porta-Potty at a construction site. He broke his way out and walked back to campus in the middle of the night. Then, college life changed for everyone.

In 1969, the military draft lottery officials notified all students that they might be required to fight in the Vietnam War when they graduated from college. Then on May 4, 1970, the Kent State University shootings occurred. Four students were killed by the Ohio State National Guard. This happened during an anti-Vietnam War rally. Duke and other universities feared violence might

Duke University Chapel

occur during similar rallies on campuses. These colleges ended the school year early before final exams were taken. John had fallen behind in his studies and had hoped to improve his grades by getting high scores on his final exams. Without being able to take these exams, however, he feared that he would not be allowed to return to Duke in the fall. John made a deal with his professors to study harder, and he was invited back for the next year. Now, he made plans for the summer.

Uncle Fred came back into the picture and offered him the same summer job John had worked the previous summer of 1969. John appreciated his kindness. Uncle Fred had created a new department at his company, CF&I, to explore for gold, silver, molybdenum, copper, and other precious metals.

John had a strong urge to travel. He and a friend decided to ride over 2,000 miles to California on motorcycles. They planned to spend the summer out there. John Sr. thought that John would not be safe riding all the way across the country. He had John strap the motorcycle flat on top of his Volkswagen Beetle's sunroof to transport it. John loved his father, but it was the dumbest thing John had ever seen. Both felt this might be more dangerous than riding to California. They took the motorcycle off the car roof. It was time to hop on the "bike" and go. As John drove off, "I remember my mother and father saying goodbye to me thinking they would never see me again. But they had always allowed me the freedom to make my own mistakes, hopefully thinking that I might learn and benefit from them." John's big plans changed quickly. One hundred miles later, his motorcycle slid in gravel off a winding mountain road and was destroyed. Fortunately, John was not seriously injured.

The Honda 450 before heading for California, June 1970

John was hired as a junior geologist and worked with 12 other geologists. He labored throughout Colorado and in other Western states. He woke up early each day and had a quick bite to eat. Then he was dropped off at a remote site at 6:00 a.m. and picked up by 7:00 p.m. His job was to make geochemical surveys by digging in the soil to discover if precious mineral deposits were located far underground. John hiked long distances with no trails in order to dig a small hole every 100 feet in an assigned area. Next, he put the dirt sample in a small manila bag. The location was marked on a map to verify where he found it. Assayers checked the samples for their mineral composition.

John worked alone in the mountains up to 13,000 feet above sea level. He endured the hot sun, thunderstorms, and even snow in the early summer. John learned how to deal with sudden changes of weather in the high country. The solitude of the mountains appealed to him. After each day's work that summer, he went back to the Snowshoe Motel in Creede, Colorado. It was time to eat, relax, and get ready for a good night's rest. While working alone both summers, John's self-reliance grew, and his outdoor skills improved. And an important part of his personality that would define the rest of his life was developing: "All of this exploring nature 'off-trail' gave me confidence while trekking in remote places, and the joy of discovering things that others never would. I would employ this courage and curiosity for the balance of my life 'going off-trail' in business, photography, environmental advocacy, even while raising my family. I suppose you could also call it 'calculated risk-taking.'" The next summer, he worked again in his father's department store. He was given additional duties and learned more about how retail business worked. His selling and marketing skills were developing.

Prospecting for silver at 13,000' in the San Juan Mountains on the Continental Divide near Creede, Colorado, August 1970

In 1972, John graduated from Duke University in four years. He had improved his grades by attending classes regularly, putting more effort into his studies, and participating in fewer pranks! "As I had suspected and hoped after high school, my college years allowed almost complete freedom to 'do my own thing' for better or worse. The boundaries of 'right and wrong' that my mother and father had created for me turned out to be just what I needed. In fact, college allowed me to continue to grow as a person, to increase my social skills, and to gain more confidence in myself and my abilities."

John chose to seek a career after college instead of going to graduate school. "I wanted to move on quickly to make a living and find financial independence from my family. I also wanted to see exactly what I could accomplish in my life. I had benefited from such an interesting and diverse background, and maybe had gained a few skills with which to be successful. The easy part was that I knew exactly where I wanted to be," he said. Within three days of graduating from Duke, John moved to Colorado. He did not know precisely what he would do. His experiences in Colorado with Mrs. Hickman, working on the ranch, and prospecting for minerals made him think that he could be happy living there for the rest of his life. "Anyway, in 1964, I had told Mrs. Hickman that I would live in Colorado someday, so I'd better do it!" John left behind family, friends, a job, and the area where he grew up. He did not have a job waiting for him in Colorado. However, his parents still believed in him. Although they would miss John, they encouraged him to follow his dream. This is not the last time John received support from them.

The graduate ready for the "real" world, Duke University, 1972

Hallett Peak at sunrise, Rocky Mountain National Park

4
CHAPTER

Into the Real World
1972 – 1981 (Ages 22-31)

Upon arrival in Colorado, John checked in with the Denver-based Fielders, Uncle Fred, Aunt Virginia, and their son, Fred, Jr., John's older cousin. Fred, Jr., nicknamed Buzz, was a district attorney who did real estate deals on the side. He immediately offered John an opportunity. Buzz helped John earn a real estate broker's license so that together they could earn commissions buying and selling ranches. Then John and Buzz talked to a group of farmers about selling their water to the federal government. These farmers mostly grew barley for the Coors Beer Company. The property was in Monte Vista, located in the scenic San Luis Valley. This valley has immense snowcapped peaks on all sides and is the size of Rhode Island. John and his cousin planned to make a lot of money from this deal. However, the federal government decided to get the water a different way. While working there, John met a lot of friendly people in the area. Years later, he got permission from them to photograph ranches for a book about saving ranchland. After struggling for a year and a half, John left the real estate business. He looked back at this time as "a valuable business experience, and a lesson in how to effectively sell my ideas to people, and to negotiate contracts."

John now wanted to succeed in the same business in which his father had excelled, retail merchandising. John got a job at the Denver Dry Goods Company department store. That building is now a historic

Sunset over the Gore Range, Summit County

Bison in the San Luis Valley with the Sangre de Cristo Mountains in the background

landmark, located in downtown Denver. Though he was paid to work five days a week, it required six to get all of the work done. John was not paid for the extra hours he worked. He thought that this would impress his bosses and lead to a promotion. His starting wage was $7,500 per year as an executive trainee. John wanted to move up to a higher position in a year or two. An idea for advancement popped into his head: Sit next to the company president at company lunches and maybe get noticed by him. John wore a nice new suit and talked with the boss. It worked! Politics and hard work got him promoted into a new job. Unfortunately, this man soon left the company, and John lost his supporter. The new president did not know John, and future promotions seemed less likely.

John left this job and got a new one at a competitor, the May D&F Department Store. He again worked hard and planned his career path. His efforts paid off. He eventually earned a high level position by the young age of 29. He became the general manager of the May D&F branch store at the original Southglenn Mall in Littleton, Colorado, where he supervised 120 employees.

One day in 1975 after joining May D&F, John heard a voice around the corner from his desk. "The person on the other side of the short wall was the most beautiful woman I had ever seen. I fell in love at first sight," he remembered. John had just met his future wife, Virginia "Gigi" Yonkers. They enjoyed each other's company and spent a lot of time together. "She was humble and thoughtful in addition to beautiful … a unique combination." Though a big city person from Chicago, she loved nature and started hiking with him in the outdoors. On weekends they took overnight camping trips. With both families in attendance, in 1978 they were married in the picturesque Sangre de Cristo Mountains near Westcliffe. This was where John had worked as a teenager on the ranch.

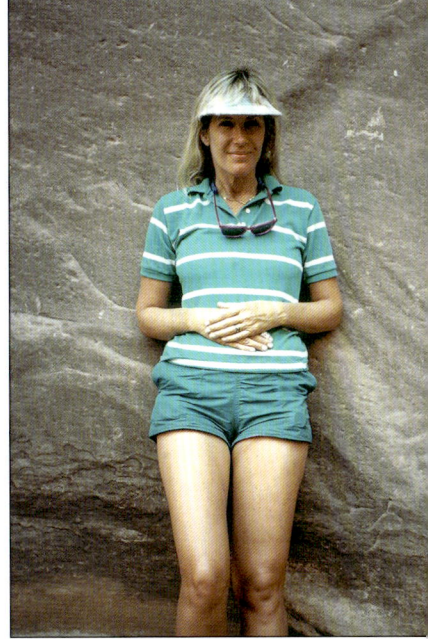

Gigi

When John first moved out to Colorado, he hiked and backpacked alone in the mountains. He liked going wherever he wanted. Though he loved climbing to the top of soaring mountain peaks, he enjoyed it more seeing those same peaks reflected in the clear alpine lakes. Cobalt blue skies complemented mountains made orange by the low-lying sun at sunrise and sunset. As always, he also wanted to share what he saw with others. He felt like a kid exclaiming, "Can you believe what I just saw?" John had painted with acrylics on canvas from 1966 to 1973. He liked painting landscapes, but taking painting supplies on hikes was difficult. How could he still capture those images? Maybe photography? Taking snapshots on school field trips and during his summers in Colorado had been fun for John.

Then he came across an inspiring book *In Wildness is the Preservation of the World* by well-known photographer Eliot Porter. "Eliot Porter was a color photographer. He lived and worked during the same part of the 20th century as Ansel Adams, who was a black and white photographer," John said. "I had never seen nature portrayed the way Porter photographed it. He avoided showing skies and horizons, preferring to photograph what he called 'the intimate landscape.' His images were filled with autumn leaves and tree trunks in New England, and lily pads on ponds tucked into dense deciduous forests. He had a way of making shapes and textures, as well as extensive palettes of color, the focus of the image. He did not need dramatic skies to create a sense of moment (photographs that capture unique light or weather). Porter had a vision that I did not have, and I was envious. I wanted to be just like him. I wanted to see those aspects of nature. I fell in love with nature photography the day that I saw Porter's book."

Gigi and John marry December 28, 1978 in Westcliffe, Colorado

In Wildness is the Preservation of the World book by Eliot Porter

Chapter Four: Into the Real World

In 1973, John rented a Pentax 35mm camera and bought the best slide film available, Kodachrome 25 (ASA 25 film produced sharp and colorful images). Soon, he purchased a Canon F-1 professional 35mm camera. It produced higher quality images. He used his day off each week and time during vacations from work to take photos. John always looked closely at Porter's book the night before he left on his

"Eliot Porter was my 'artistic' photographer hero. Ansel Adams, though as much the artist as Porter, was my 'environmentalist' photographer hero. He photographed mostly with black and white film. In the history of American conservation, few people had worked as long and as effectively to preserve wilderness as Ansel Adams. Through his photographs, he touched countless people with a sense of the mystery of what lies unseen in wild places. In addition, he was an activist and personally lobbied congressmen, cabinet officers, and Presidents on behalf of wilderness values. He set the example for me that I could make the world a better place with my own photographs." Though John preferred photographing in color all of his life, in 2018 he published his first book of black and white images, *Colorado Black on White*. To make the book, John selected 230 images from his life's work and turned them into black and white on his computer.

Ansel Adams' most famous photograph, "Moonrise, Hernandez, New Mexico, 1941." "Most people do not realize that this photograph was made in broad daylight. Using filters on his camera and print-making techniques, he made daytime look like nighttime. This is why he was an artist. He 'saw' the picture in his mind before he actually took the photograph!"

photography trips. Keeping those images in mind helped John see nature better and compose good scenes.

While John worked at The Denver Dry Goods store, he used their photography shop that processed film. John dropped off his Kodachrome there on Monday mornings and picked up the slides by Friday. He examined the pictures closely to see how they turned out. At first, the pictures didn't look at all like Porter's. "What was I doing wrong?" I asked myself. "Eventually, I figured out that our eyes see differently than the camera and film. The one eye of the camera lens cannot portray depth in a scene in the same way we see with two eyes. And film cannot capture detail in highlight and shadow areas simultaneously as effectively as our eyes. This handicap became my friend when I learned how to compose those dark shadows into my designs. I also learned that Porter photographed mostly in cloudy light in order to eliminate this contrast problem completely. This also rendered his colors more saturated and genuine." John's pictures started to look similar to Porter's images. But he was only copying Porter. He did not think that his photographs reflected his personal experiences in nature. It would take more practice to do that.

The Canon F-1 35mm camera and 35mm roll film.

A good example of "contrasty" transparency film, Weminuche Wilderness, San Juan Mountains

Chapter Four: Into the Real World

John often photographed in locations at least a few hours' drive from home. He prepared his equipment and food the night before leaving. The next morning, John's alarm went off early. He dragged himself out of bed, trudged out the door, and started driving at 2:00 a.m. in order to get to the trailhead (where the trail starts) before sunrise. He owned a 1971 Toyota Corolla. This drove well on paved streets but was not built to deal with rough unpaved roads which led to the remote trailheads. He taped his ankles with athletic tape (the same as he had done playing football and basketball) to avoid sprains. Then he ran several miles up the trail with camera, food, and water in a small backpack. This included a steep climb of 3,000 feet in elevation from 8,500 to 11,500 feet above sea level. He hoped to arrive at the photo location by 5:30 a.m. On this trip, he wanted to catch the perfect light of sunrise on the Sangre de Cristo Mountains. The low angle of the sun enhanced the colors and shadows. Taking pictures and experiencing nature were high priorities for John. Much effort was put into these journeys. Surprisingly, he discovered that he enjoyed the solitude and being alone in nature even more than he enjoyed taking pictures!

John learned how to drive the Toyota on roads that only Jeeps might take. On more than one occasion, he drove it on the rugged four-wheel-drive road to the top of Engineer Pass at 12,800 feet. John drove slowly over and beside large rocks and deep gullies. The exhaust pipe broke more than once when it hit rocks. John was persistent about getting to picturesque places to take photos. By 1975 he was earning enough money to buy a Chevy Blazer four-wheel-drive vehicle. Now

Running up and down the Sangre de Cristo Mountains in Adidas "Country" cross country running shoes. In the early 1970s, there were only three such shoe models available for running on trails!

Gigi and the Chevy Blazer. Now John could finally drive the very worst of roads.

he went to destinations he couldn't go to with his small Toyota. From 1973 to 1981, limited time off from work prevented multi-day backpacking trips. As he learned his new craft, John traveled on much of Colorado's extensive network of old mining roads.

Photographer David Muench's work inspired John's photography career. Muench's exquisite landscape photos and pictures in remote areas caught John's attention. These were taken with a 4x5 view camera, the kind of camera where under a dark cloth, you extend the bellows (accordion-like part) to focus the lens on a piece of frosted glass. And the image you see is upside down! In order to produce the highest quality photos, John bought this type of camera midway during his department store career. Now, his large 4" x 5" transparencies (slides) could have the depth and clarity of professional photographers. The camera used several lenses and other pieces of equipment. This was the beginning of many years of lugging 65 pounds of photography equipment in a special camera backpack. Over time, he hiked thousands of miles in rugged country. This strenuous exercise contributed to John having surgery later in life to have one hip and both knees replaced with artificial metal joints!

John taught himself how to be a photographer. He learned how to use the camera by reading books. "I didn't have the time and resources to attend workshops and take lessons," he said. "I had to learn photography by trial and error, and by studying the books of other photographers I admired. The more I photographed, like anything in life, the better I got. More importantly, the more I explored, the more I saw. I like to say to young photographers: 'If you can't see it, you can't photograph it.' And I was careful to both recognize and admit my mistakes. I also understood that it was important to give myself credit for the successful images."

John persisted and succeeded at taking magnificent photographs. However, another area of his life was not going as well. John was not satisfied with department store work. Being a manager was not a good fit for him. He didn't like supervising so many employees. He was discovering that his independent personality was better suited to be

The large format German Linhof view camera that John used for 25 years

an entrepreneur, someone who works on his own. In addition, his passion for spending time in the outdoors was growing. These things influenced a risky business decision he was about to make. In the meantime, Gigi made a critical choice. When she met John, they both were assistant buyers at the store, and she too had career plans. After she and John married, however, having a family became more important. In 1980, John and Gigi had their son John Thomas "JT" Fielder, III. By 1981, they were expecting another child, Ashley.

San Juan Mountains in the fall near Telluride, Colorado

John thought about leaving the department store business and starting a career in photography. He wanted to experience the freedom, risk, and rewards of running his own business. Gigi did not agree with this at first. She and John talked a lot about this career change. Leaving a high-paying secure job and expecting a child at the same time to start a new business was risky. So, they made an agreement: He would try photography for one year. If it didn't work out, John would return to department store work. John wanted to make a living out of a career that many people would like to have, but at which very few succeed!

Support from John's parents and siblings was essential, and John recalled that "when I quit my job to turn my passion into a career, Dad never discouraged me. He never said that this was a risk not worth taking. He did advise me to have back-up plans and to have enough money to get started. Then he asked if he could help." These words inspired John to start his new business. John left the department store and began his photography career. He took a big risk to do something for which he had a great passion. John greatly appreciated both his father's and Gigi's selfless support of him in his decision.

Waterfall, Middle Fork Conejos River, South San Juan Wilderness

5
CHAPTER

A New Career
1981-2019 (Ages 32-69)

"By now I felt that my previous path in life made it my destiny to be a nature photographer," John stated. "That made the decision much easier to quit my high-paying job and the security it gave me and my family. Clearly, the influences in my life had determined my path forward: experiencing nature at Camp Sequoya from 1960 to 1963, Mrs. Hickman leading those summer trips in 1963 and 1964, Mr. Birch instilling in me an appreciation for art and personal expression in 1967 and 1968, and Uncle Fred finding those summer jobs for me in Colorado."

His growing family was depending on John to succeed in his new career. He spent the first six months figuring out how to get the business started. "Do I open a gallery and sell prints for the wall or publish books like David Muench?" he asked himself. Muench's Colorado photographs appeared in beautiful, large coffee-table-style books. "I decided to skip the gallery business for the time being and try to publish similar books, and calendars like those printed by Sierra Club." Most of the existing Colorado calendars had average quality photos. To get started, John wanted to publish a superior calendar for a higher price. Was this a good business plan?

A person needs money to buy equipment or services to begin a business. John's father, ever supportive and generous, loaned him

Fresh snow, Daniels Park, Douglas County

$15,000 to start a company called Western Images. He had faith in John's abilities. A Denver offset printer charged that amount to print 10,000 Colorado 1982 scenic calendars. John had a business plan for selling the calendars. That summer of 1981, he personally visited 135 bookstores and gift shops in Colorado. During each visit, he asked, "Would you sell this calendar for me?" Every store but one said yes. John delivered all of the calendars to the stores in the fall. Then he thought, "Maybe I won't have enough for Christmas reorders." He printed 5,000 more calendars. Unfortunately, John overestimated demand.

The 1982 Colorado scenic wall calendar

Calendars sell best between Thanksgiving and Christmas, but by the end of the year, he had 4,000 calendars left over! Most of his profits were wiped out. John had made the first of many mistakes in publishing. From this one, he learned that calendars sell mostly in December at retail. The clock was ticking on his one-year agreement with Gigi. He had proved that there was demand for a higher-quality Colorado photographic product, but he made a miscalculation and wasted his profits. Nevertheless, he had learned in life to both admit his mistakes and to recognize his successes. He would not make the same error again.

This setback taught John how to deal with adversity. It was against the odds to succeed quickly while making a dramatic switch in careers. Some people told him that it might be impossible to make a good living from nature photography. John was determined to succeed, and he was not discouraged. His photography career dream would come true. Plus, he had a family to feed. It was time to try a new strategy.

John said to himself, "I don't have much money, but now I know all the retail gift shops and bookstores. People are beginning to talk favorably about John Fielder and his photos. So, how do I move forward with my new career?" He developed a new business plan which included publishing calendars yearly and his first book. But he needed a lot more money than before to get started. His cousin Buzz introduced John to an investor who had done well in the magazine business. John asked him to pay the costs of publishing a large book in return for a share of the company profits. The plan also included publishing nature books and calendars in other states. He started a new publishing company, Westcliffe Publishers, and used his garage as the warehouse. It was named after the first place he had photographed in Colorado. He hired sales representatives to sell to stores, graphic designers to put pictures and text together artistically, editors to rewrite the text, and printers. In 1982, he published his first large-format book, *Colorado Hidden Valleys*.

John's first "coffee table" book

John wanted to expand his inventory, so he traveled and took photographs in Washington and California, in addition to Colorado. He and his family even spent the summer of 1985 in the state of Washington. John backpacked and photographed the Cascade Mountains and the coast of the Pacific Ocean. But he quickly discovered that running a publishing company was very demanding. He only had enough time to photograph in Colorado. So, he hired highly regarded landscape photographers to take pictures in 35 other states. John edited the photographers' images, and his staff published the books and calendars. For the next 25 years, Westcliffe published several hundred book titles, including 40 of John's. It also produced calendars representing

Some of the other books that John published over the years

the states. With this business plan, he began to make a comfortable living and support the family.

To build the business for himself and his partner, John used extensive planning, perseverance, and an entrepreneurial spirit. He applied many skills learned in college. And John Sr. and Uncle Fred had set the right examples for John to be successful. "I inherited the organizational skills, common sense, and ability to prioritize from my father," he admitted. "You must have a good plan, and a backup plan since things do not always happen the way you expect. I had learned this the hard way dealing with things such as the bad weather that Mother Nature threw at me while photographing. More important than all these things was a strong desire to succeed and passion for what

Backcountry skiing and photographing the Sneffels Range, 1988

Chapter Five: A New Career   49

I was doing. And I was making the world a better place by showing people the glory of nature." The tremendous support Gigi gave to John and their family made his success possible. In 2007, with the family grown up and out of the home, John sold Westcliffe Publishers to another company. He moved from the Front Range of Colorado to the mountains of Summit County. In 2009, he started John Fielder Publishing company to continue publishing his annual calendars, and a new book almost every year.

John has made his living as a nature photographer from book and calendar publishing and by teaching photography workshops. Though he decided in 1981 not to try to make a living from selling framed photographs, he eventually did produce prints for sale in galleries. In 2002, he opened his own gallery, John Fielder's Colorado, in the Cherry Creek Shopping Center in Denver. Expensive rents led him to close it in 2006. That same year he reopened the gallery at 833 Santa Fe Drive in the Art District on Santa Fe in Denver. He closed that space in 2017 in order to reduce the amount of time he was spending in Denver.

"When you live in paradise (Summit County), it is difficult to come to the city," John said. "Over the years, the sights and sounds of nature have become more appealing to me than the noises and smells of the city!"

John Fielder's Colorado gallery in the Cherry Creek Mall, 2002

JohnFielder.com

John continues to sell his books, fine art prints, as well as photography workshops, on his website **www.johnfielder.com**. The website also lists the complete schedule of his workshops and entertaining slide shows. There are even 1,000 images online for visitors to browse through, if not purchase as a print. Today's nature photographers must take full advantage of the digital world in order to have any hope of making a living. This includes website development, social media, and search engine marketing. John dabbles in these things and regularly promises his fans that he will become more socially outgoing, but it never seems to happen! John's books and calendars are also sold by bookstores, gift shops, and online retailers such as Amazon.

Red-tailed hawk flies through a rainbow, San Juan National Forest

6
CHAPTER

John
the Family Man

John grew up in a nurturing family environment. Everyone in his family worked hard, played hard, and they enjoyed many activities together. John's family vacationed together, even after the four children had left home, for 35 years at the beach in South Carolina. "We enjoyed playing golf, tennis, and spending time under the sun together. It was a lovely family existence for the six of us," John recalled. "Mom loved cooking her homegrown vegetables for everyone and enjoyed treating family and friends like royalty. She joyfully participated in these outings until the end of her life, and like my dad, was a wonderful influence on me."

The annual family summer vacation at North Litchfield Beach, South Carolina
Opposite: Rosy paintbrush wildflowers below Capitol Peak, Maroon Bells-Snowmass Wilderness

As a parent himself, John believed that, "the example you set is far more important than what you say." John's highest personal priority was taking care of and spending time with his family. He also worked hard to build his photography and publishing business. John added staff to the publishing company so he could spend more time with family. "Gigi was incredibly supportive and a great stay-at-home mom." She enthusiastically raised their three children, JT, Ashley, and Katy, who was born in 1985.

After returning from a photography trip on a Friday, John spent the weekend with the family. Getting hugs from everyone when he got home was heartwarming. After a week of "trail food," he loved tasty home cooked meals. He enthusiastically attended his children's school activities and sports events. "Family was a huge part of my existence. I could not be alone for a week or two in the wilderness, and be a content, happy person, without a family to come home to," he admitted.

JT, Katy, and Ashley. "JT was our oldest child. He was a sweet little boy who evolved into a happy and successful young man. He grew tall like my dad and me. JT loved his mother and sisters very much. He looked out for the girls as they grew up, and they looked up to him as their 'cool' big brother. Ashley was two years younger than JT. She is blond and tall. She was a good student who inherited a bit of her dad's ambitiousness. She became a successful television anchor and reporter before starting her family. Katy was four years younger than Ashley, blue-eyed like her mom, and the 'baby' in the family. The age gap was probably one reason why she inherited a bit of her dad's independent spirit and introspective personality. She, too, was a good student who became a successful marketing executive for technology companies."

1986: "We were on a July family car camping trip to the San Juan Mountains. The first night we set up tents outside our Toyota Land Cruiser wagon parked in the La Plata Mountains, northwest of Durango. The next day I decided to drive the family up the precipitous Kennebec Pass road to 11,683 feet above sea level. A cliff was above us on one side and a cliff straight down 500 feet on the other side. The views from on top of the pass were amazing. However, there was still some snow in the road ruts. On the way down the pass, the left front tire hit some old snow and forced the steering wheel to turn to the left. The vehicle skidded, and the left front wheel was suspended in outer space over the cliff. Luckily, the other three wheels were planted on the road.

Gigi was sitting up front and the three kids in the back seat. I immediately told the family to slowly exit the vehicle on the uphill side. Without Gigi's weight in the front passenger seat, the imbalance might be just enough to cause the Toyota to roll down the mountain! I was sitting on the downhill side and would not be able to get out at the last second if it did roll. Well...it did not roll! I shifted the vehicle into the low-low 4-wheel drive gear and put the transmission into reverse. Would three of four tires on the ground create enough traction to pull back the left front tire from hanging over the edge? It worked! Totally relieved I backed up, reloaded the family, and we headed down the mountain to our next car camping site."

If you look closely, you can see the children in the back seat of the Toyota on the way up the Kennebec Pass road

Family llama expedition to Yule Lakes in the Raggeds Wilderness near Crested Butte, Colorado

John and Gigi delighted in taking their children on outdoor trips. They eagerly shared their enjoyment of nature with them when they were young. Even though she grew up in a big city, Gigi had become a fine outdoorswoman. When John pushed the kids too fast or too far, she always came to their rescue and made "dad" slow down! Strong family bonds were built during these family excursions into the woods. They created many fond memories.

It was quite the expedition when the Fielder family hiked deep into the woods. They used three llamas to carry the camping equipment, food for five people, and 65 pounds of camera equipment. John carried two-year-old Katy in a Gerry pack on his back. The other two kids and Gigi led three llamas. The llamas usually followed John's directions, but sometimes they didn't cooperate. They had a mind of their own. The family also laughed at the unusual things the llamas did, like spitting at each other when annoyed. Everyone had many playful conversations and took pleasure in each other's company as they walked through

Family llama expedition to Peeler Basin near Crested Butte, Colorado

Rafting the Dolores River in southwestern Colorado

amazingly beautiful areas. Often, the family hiked six to seven miles each day and camped out for three or more days. As busy as John's schedule was, this solitary time with the family was especially important to him.

The Fielder family also loved going river rafting. Shoving off the riverbank into the flowing water was a thrill. They floated peacefully in some places. In other areas, John masterfully steered the boat around boulders and through turbulent whitewater rapids. After floating downstream for miles, they found a good landing spot in a clearing along the edge of the bank. Then, the kids jumped out of the boat, ran around on shore, played with tadpoles, dug in the sand, and explored. John and Gigi sat in chairs snacking and relaxing, often with margaritas in hand. As the seasons changed, the Fielders also had fun in the cold weather.

John's family jumped into winter skiing in a big way. They skied at resorts and to remote huts on overnight excursions. While backcountry skiing, John pulled little Katy in a sled attached to his waist. When each child was six years old, John found them Norwegian children's cross-country skis. Gliding along quietly in the snow while looking at the mountain scenery was invigorating. They had a great time skiing up to six miles to remote huts, often climbing more than two thousand vertical feet up the mountain. At other times the family stayed in comfortable hotels during spring break, such as the old Grand Butte Hotel in Crested Butte. Here they learned how to downhill ski. It was thrilling with all five family members going down the mountain so fast side by side. John and his family were enjoying life to the fullest. Then things changed dramatically.

Skiing to the old mining town of Gothic near Crested Butte, Colorado

In 1998 John's family experienced heartbreak. John and Gigi's friends noticed that she had been losing some of her memory skills. When these symptoms worsened, John persistently took Gigi to several doctors and medical specialists. He was adamant about learning if this was a medical problem. After extensive testing, Gigi was found to have early onset (beginning at an early age) of Alzheimer's disease. She was only 52 years old. John faced a serious predicament. People with this disease must be given a lot of help to perform life's basic skills. His adolescent children needed extra attention and support. Gigi's medical costs and other family expenses would begin to pile up. What to do? Many family adjustments had to be made.

Katy and her favorite llama, Tommie

Soon after the diagnosis was confirmed, John talked with his children, ages 12, 16, and 18, at the dinner table one night. "Your mom," he told them, "has Alzheimer's disease." They knew their mom was sick but did not know it was that serious. "The kids and I discussed how to take good care of her, which we decided was the most important thing. We also needed to be aware of the impact that her illness could have on our own quality of life. My organizational skills took over. I needed to do well for Gigi, but at the same time, I had to manage the busiest years of my career. I needed to make money to support Gigi, her care, and pay for family needs, including JT's college expenses."

"We acknowledged that for the rest of our lives, we would be different people than if Gigi's illness had not happened. Hopefully, we could become better people while dealing with adversity, become more thoughtful, more compassionate to others, and be better able to deal with future crises. We also agreed to keep doing the things in life that we all enjoyed, like exploring nature. We agreed that we would have good attitudes and try to make a 'positive' out of a 'negative.'"

Enjoying the Pawnee Buttes in eastern Colorado, the Great Plains

It was a hectic time for the family. The children were busy with school, sports, and social activities. Gigi could not even drive the kids to their school activities or be available emotionally for them. Within two years, Gigi lost the ability to communicate with language. Her communication now was hugs, kisses, and smiles. Sometimes the children felt stigmatized because their mom had Alzheimer's, and they did not want to share what was happening with their friends. She was "different" than the other mothers. Even though JT was away at college, he also felt the considerable effects of his mom's illness. However, in spite of her declining health, Gigi was going to live the rest of her life in the comfort of her home. John had made the decision in the beginning not to place her in an institution. The combined caregiving skills of close friends, the three children, full and part time employees, and John, provided Gigi with the quality of life that she deserved.

The Fielders continued to travel with Gigi even when Gigi was affected by Alzheimer's disease, Puako, Hawaii

In September 2005, after seven years with Alzheimer's disease, Gigi passed away quietly in her home. John and the children were deeply affected. "We knew that Gigi's death would be the end of the natural process of this degenerative disease and not as much of a shock, but it was still very difficult," John said. "Now we needed to focus on returning to more normal lives. We had to appreciate what we had in our lives, not what we did not have: a mom and a wife." Not long before this, the family had grieved another major family loss. John's father passed away in November 2004.

During his mother's illness, JT attended Colorado State University and the University of Colorado at Boulder. He made many friends and was a good athlete and accomplished outdoorsman. JT and his friends from high school and college had been John's "sherpas" (a term borrowed from the Himalayan race of people named Sherpa) for many summers. They carried sleeping bags, tents, food, and other supplies. Then, at the age of 26, he suffered a significant chest injury while skiing at Snowmass Mountain. This required a four-hour surgery to repair the damage. JT worked hard for months on his physical therapy to recover, but he wasn't improving. He wondered if he would ever be the same.

Gigi and JT

During this period of doubt, JT worked at the Izze Beverage Company in Boulder. When laid off from his job, he felt much disappointment. There also was sadness about recently breaking up with his girlfriend. He felt terrible about the lack of recovery from the ski injury. Worse yet, JT experienced much grief about his mom passing away five months before. Tragedy struck the family again. In March 2006, he skied to the top of 12,000-foot Butler Gulch below Berthoud

Pass. At age 26, he took his own life there on the mountaintop. Gigi's death was expected. JT's death was a complete shock.

This was an incredible amount of family loss within a short time span. "How do you psychologically deal with so much trauma? How do you help two daughters deal with losing their mom and brother within six months?" John asked himself. "I had to learn how to deal with my own mental health and at the same time nurture those around me. I thought that I had already dealt with great adversity, but now it rose to an even higher level."

JT Fielder

John received counseling for six months from a psychologist who was a friend of the family. "When you have such things happen to you, only friends, family, and counseling can begin to cure the pain," John said. "Ironically, although being in nature was always a source of healing for me, in this case, being alone outdoors was not a solution." Ultimately, only the passage of time helped John with his healing. He took extra care of his family and concentrated on his work. He and his daughters pulled together to make it through this immensely difficult time.

"We think about JT and Gigi every day of our lives and feel pain from the losses. But both episodes taught us that life is both rewarding and tragic, not just for us, but for everyone. It is the way life is. Perspective is everything. Without loss, you cannot appreciate gain. Joy is more intense when you know sadness. We acknowledged that our losses were terrible, but perhaps less than those of other families in even more difficult situations around the world. In part because of losing a mom and brother, Ashley and Katy have become remark-

Chapter Six: John, the Family Man

able young women, more compassionate and unselfish than they would have been otherwise. And my daughters are experiencing the joy of producing the descendants of Gigi and JT."

Since he was well known, John was asked by the Alzheimer's and mental health communities

The first day of kindergarten for Virginia Carolyn Visser, Gigi, Ashley's oldest child, 2016

Ashley, John, and Katy at the Carson J. Spencer Foundation annual fundraising event at which John received an award for his work promoting suicide prevention

Ashley, Daniel, Savannah, Dan, Gigi, Joe, Katy, John, Brother Bill, sister-in-law Vicki, Telluride, 2018

to speak about his family losses. He spent much time talking to the public about these issues. This raised money and awareness for organizations treating people suffering from similar conditions.

John is thankful that his daughters have an appreciation for nature and are protective of it. They will pass this on to the next Fielder generation. Ashley has four children whose ages are seven, five, two, and Isla, who was born in May 2019. Katy married in 2018 in Telluride, Colorado. She is starting her own family. Both daughters married wonderful men who are athletes and outdoorsmen.

In 2007 John moved to a new home in Summit County. He made a cardboard model of a 19th-century Colorado mining stamp mill, where ore is crushed to dust using a heavy "stamp" or hammer, and had his house built to look like it. It is made of recycled barnwood and rusty corrugated metal and resembles the old mine buildings he has discovered and photographed for 40 years. A solar panel provides all of his electricity. His home is located on an aspen-covered mountain-

John's home in the Williams Fork Mountains, Summit County

side high above the lower Blue River Valley, and it faces west towards the rugged Gore Range. There is a breathtaking view of the valley bounded by 13,000-foot high mountains on both sides.

John's house has a mix of landscape photos and artists' paintings on the walls. There are numerous photos of his family lined up on top of a display case. Though he generally disapproves of "taking" things out of nature, John also keeps a handful of "found" items on display. On one piece of furniture lay the artifacts from the Temple of the Sun, a doll from Namibia, coral from Hawaii, and the horn of a Colorado bighorn sheep. The serenity of his home makes it a place to contemplate and rejuvenate.

John and Brother Bill use a llama "caddy" to carry golf clubs at the Crested Butte Golf Club. They were asked to leave the course after playing 6 holes, 1993

John travels half of the year. When he is home, John enjoys reading: spy novels, mysteries, science and nature books, and current articles about the state of Earth's health and biodiversity. World War II history is especially interesting to John. He is also a student of quantum mechanics. "Quantum physics is a passion … the size and mystery of the universe allow me to better appreciate our earthly existence," he said. Every day of my life I try to acknowledge how lucky I am to exist, be a sentient human being with arms, legs, and a head!" John hides a smile when he says that "just as importantly," he is a big sports and car racing fan, and he likes to play golf with friends and family.

John worked hard to make a productive life for himself and his family. John's true wealth is in his family and the appreciation of nature. He enjoys the solitude of the outdoors and loves the company of his family. One measure of John's success is how well he has balanced family, nature, and photography.

7
CHAPTER

John
the Photographer

John feels confident about his skill as a photographer. As a lifelong learner though, he continues to want to improve. He relies upon his still deepening relationship with nature to provide new ways to portray it in a photograph. The more he explores, the more he sees. As a result, when John returns to a place he photographed 30 years ago, he takes far more images than the first time. He is quick to admit that making good images is not all about talent: "Successful photography is a function of two things, each of exactly the same proportion: having a good eye (seeing clearly how subjects, color, lighting, and objects in a picture fit together) and being at the right place at the right time." John's greatest passion is nature, second is photography. He has always avoided photographing iconic, that is, well-known places, in favor of less visited, more remote locations. John's relationship with nature is very personal, and he is distracted standing near other photographers, even other people, when he photographs.

John takes pictures throughout the year. Each season has its rewards and challenges for photography. In the spring, flowers are blooming, trees have lime-green leaves, and rivers and streams are gushing with icy cold water. Most of the tall peaks have white mantels of snow on them contrasting against the deep blue sky. In summer, trees and vegetation leaf out. The aspen leaves "quake" (hence aspens are called "quakies") in the breezes, and wind whistles through the pines.

Lupine wildflowers, Gunnison National Forest

Water is still flowing in the streams and rivers. In the fall, the aspen leaves turn yellow-gold, even orange and red, and provide a colorful contrast to the complimentary blue sky. Snow is starting to layer the upper elevations. There's less water running in streams and rivers. In winter, snow contrasts with the granite peaks and dark evergreens. The lakes and streams are frozen. It is the world of white.

John uses a variety of methods of travel and different equipment to explore and photograph. In the spring he enjoys rafting through magnificent sandstone canyons when the melting winter snowpack swells the rivers. His SUV tows his raft to "put-in" locations along the rivers. Friends then help John "shuttle" his SUV and trailer to the "take-out" location many miles downstream. In summer, John tows a durable llama trailer with his SUV. They go on rugged four-wheel drive roads to remote wilderness trailheads. John saddles two llamas

John loves how a single Colorado place changes from one season to the next. The Double RL Ranch near Ridgway, Colorado

Chapter Seven: John, the Photographer

One of the highlights of John's career was photographing the entire Rocky Mountain National Park in 1993 and 1994, all 358 square miles, which is 229,000 acres! The superintendent of the park gave John a special permit never given to anyone before. John and his helpers were allowed to backpack and camp wherever they wished for two years. Normally, camping is only permitted in designated sites in the park, all of which are in the forests. John loves taking pictures of mountains reflecting in high alpine lakes. During the two summers, John camped at and photographed over 150 lakes in the park. The group hiked and bushwhacked (pushed their way through forests and thickets of willows) away from trails most of the time. Trails do not go up the steepest creek valleys and to the highest lakes in the park. To get from one high lake to another, they would scramble on the big boulders that cover mountains at 13,000 feet above sea level. Some days they hiked 15 miles and went up and down 10,000 vertical feet! In return for this permission, John gave the park copies of 1,000 of his photographs to keep as a scientific record of the park's ecology.

"My single favorite photograph depicts a remote group of alpine ponds in Rocky Mountain National Park. It is a very difficult place to find. There are no trails, and it is a long distance from anywhere! It is the most beautiful place I have ever been."

Llamas and "sherpas" in the San Juan Mountains

Pulling on the oars!

and hangs packs on their sides, and each llama carries 85 pounds of camping gear, supplies, and photography equipment. Llamas are easy to get along with and need no extra food. "The wilderness meadows are one big salad for a llama!" John says.

In the fall, John drives on remote roads through colorful aspen forests and along rivers lined with cottonwood trees turning orange. Sometimes he uses the llamas to access these forests during autumn. More often than not, though, he takes a break from the hard work of packing and hiking by just photographing along roads and sleeping in the SUV! In winter John uses "alpine touring" skis to go uphill to remote backcountry huts that he rents nightly. Staying in these cozy cabins makes photographing in cold and snowy conditions much easier.

Though John loves his solitude, winter trips can be treacherous when the snow is unstable and there is the risk of dangerous avalanches. Therefore, he usually skis with friends.

Skiing high in the Sneffels Range near Ridgway, Colorado

Photographing from the car during the fall

JT and his friends at a San Juan Mountains' campsite

John leads his "sherpas" across a steep slope of summer snow

Chapter Seven: John, the Photographer

John takes a tremendous amount of photography and camping equipment on his photo excursions, though much less now with the use of digital cameras. And he only takes what he needs. Too much gear is a distraction to his photography. For 25 years he recruited young people (and older ones, too) during the summers to carry support gear. As mentioned before, they were usually husky high school and college-age kids, including his son JT and his schoolmates. They hauled food, sleeping bags and pads, tents, and emergency equipment in 75-pound backpacks. It required four or five "sherpas" to lug the equipment and food needed for a week-long expedition into the wilderness.

In those days John used a large format film camera named a Linhof. The transparency (slide) film measured 4" x 5." It provided great detail in his photographs. In addition, he carried seven lenses, various filters, a hand-held light meter, 30 film holders, and boxes filled with 500 sheets of film. All of this fit into a specially designed camera backpack with a tripod inserted into an outside sleeve. The whole thing weighed 65 pounds. It never got lighter during the week like the other packs holding food! John switched to

Large format sheets of exposed film on which the pictures had been taken had to be replaced with unexposed film. Usually, this was done at night in the tent, but sometimes it happened in daylight inside a light-tight "changing bag" on the trail!

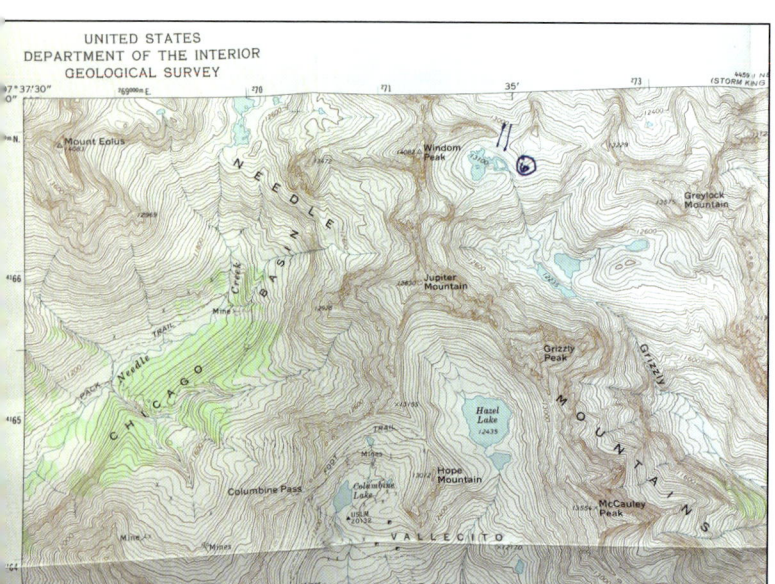

A topographic map shows the steepness of the mountains with brown contour lines and high lakes and creeks in blue. Notice John's note indicating a high mountain pass he thinks he can cross.

lighter weight digital cameras in 2010 because he realized, "By that time the quality of digital photographs had overtaken that of film cameras."

Before he leaves on an excursion into the backcountry, John looks closely at detailed topographical maps of the river canyons and mountains. These show the steepness and elevation of the terrain, and also vegetation. The maps indicate where he can hike and camp. From the maps, he can imagine what a place might look like before he actually arrives. Thorough geographical planning helps ensure the photographic success of a trip.

Before each trip, John carefully checks to make sure the camera and camping equipment work. He inspects his vehicle before his photography outings take him on long, bumpy drives. Proper preparation also improves the chances of photographic success and decreases the chances of disaster in the middle of nowhere. A checklist ensures that nothing is left behind. Imagine what life would be like in the wilderness without a backpacking stove to prepare hot food and coffee! John no longer carries heavy backpacks. His doctor says that his artificial knees and hip will last longer! John now rents llamas for the summer and fall trips. John jokes "I use rent-a-llama.com." The beasts' physical conditioning (ability to carry heavy loads for miles) must be confirmed before the summer packing season begins in July.

If John is too hot, cold, wet, tired, or hungry, he is distracted from making good photographs. Discomfort interferes with his picture taking ability and creativity. "The quality of clothing and boots I wear is critical to being comfortable in challenging weather," he said. "Boots must be waterproof and clothing water-resistant, yet breathable. The quality of my raingear must be the best available. Sleeping pads must be lightweight but comfortable and sleeping bags lightweight yet warm enough for a winter bivouac (temporary camp). Tents need to be water and windproof. My food must be tasty and full of fat for the energy necessary to hike long distances up and down mountains."

Cooking a ramen noodle with canned chicken and cream cheese dinner in the mountains!

When John arrives at a potential photo location and campsite, usually by late afternoon, he studies the landscape. He imagines what the lighting will be during the "magic" hours: one hour before sunset, as well as

John and a helper climbed from 12,000' in the dark at 4 a.m. to reach the top of Hagues Peak (13,560') before the sun rises, Rocky Mountain National Park

one hour after sunrise the next day. He thinks about and remembers potential photo compositions (how things are arranged in a picture) based upon the lay of the land. He searches for the best flowers, lichens on rocks, cascades of water, and reflections of mountains in lakes. It's important to predict where the sun will hit the mountains at sunset and sunrise. He sets up a camera on top of the tripod, his three-legged camera stand, for sunset and sunrise photographs when the light is low and camera exposures are long. Sometimes his exposures take two seconds. The tripod keeps the camera steady, so the picture is in focus.

Half of John's pictures are planned. The other half of the images are taken on the "spur of the moment" as soon as he discovers a good composition. A new "moment" can be different than any picture he has taken before, and he still experiences them, even after 40 years!

Designing a photograph with his point & shoot camera. John uses smaller cameras for his wildflower close-ups.

Chapter Seven: John, the Photographer 77

It is usually different because the location, or lighting, or cloud cover, or the weather, is not like any he has ever seen. "Quality of light is determined by the weather and the angle of the sun in the sky," he explained. "Unique light is often temporary. Therefore, I must work quickly to operate the camera in order to capture the moment. No matter how quickly I am forced to work, the most important thing is always the composition of the

Inconvenient things happen when you are exploring the wilderness. John has had to solve considerable problems or self-rescue himself over 100 times in his life. John is clearheaded in difficult circumstances. "I've been safe during these situations because I do not panic, and I enjoy the challenge of problem-solving." In 2018 alone, he endured two difficult situations. John had to get himself, a sick llama, and 200 pounds of gear, out of a remote part of Colorado's Uncompahgre Wilderness near Lake City. Then he broke the axle on his trailer while leaving to go home. A week later, he flipped his raft upside down in a dangerous whitewater rapid in the Colorado River. John lost all of his camera gear during that episode. Then in January 2019, he triggered the first avalanche of his life on a ski hut trip. The snow slide came right at him at a high speed. John was able to ski away faster than the snow and avoid being buried and injured.

John's raft is "wrapped" (stuck sideways) on a rock in the middle of Class IV-V (dangerous!) Snaggletooth Rapid in the Dolores River of southwest Colorado. From shore, other rafters are trying to pull the raft off the rock with a rope and pulleys. The raft is filled with water, and the pressure of the flowing water is great. It required several people pulling on the rope to get John and the raft off the rock.

image. I am trying to make a beautiful painting with a camera. After 40 years, designing a good photograph has become easier, and I can do it without thinking about it." Some people think photographers are very patient and will wait for better light. John is not that way. If he does not like the light or the landscape where he is, he hikes quickly down the trail or drives "way too fast in the SUV" he says, in order to find a better time and place!

John is adamant about being safe in the woods. He loves his family and has much to live for! Traveling in the rugged backcountry is always risky, especially when alone. Above all else, he conducts himself in a very conservative manner, always choosing to avoid risk over getting the "ultimate" photograph. In 45 years exploring wild places, John has never had a major injury.

John enjoys sharing his enthusiasm for nature and photography by teaching photography workshops. He and the class participants reach photogenic locations by driving, hiking, or rafting. John especially likes to instruct beginning and intermediate level photographers. "They do not think they already know it all," he said. "I can easily break bad

Working in the field with students

Chapter Seven: John, the Photographer 79

Teaching photography in the classroom

habits and share with them the 'tricks of the trade' I have learned by trial and error." He also talks passionately about protecting nature at the workshops. This is a perfect place to speak about preservation since the classes are held in scenic locations worthy of being saved.

John has published 50 books; all but three are about Colorado, and most are nature oriented. He is best known for his "then & now" history books about Colorado. John contemplated a worthwhile book project to commemorate the millennium change in 2000. He imagined what it might be like to compare Colorado in the 19th century, when it was first settled by white people, to what it looked like in 2000. He discovered that a man named W.H. Jackson had photographed Colorado and the West from 1869 to 1908. Better yet, most of Jackson's photographs were stored at the Colorado History Museum in Denver. This led to the project during which John found 300 of Jackson's original Colorado photo locations. He took the same photo all over

Volumes I and II of *Colorado 1870-2000*. Almost all of the 300 repeat photo pairs are published between the two books.

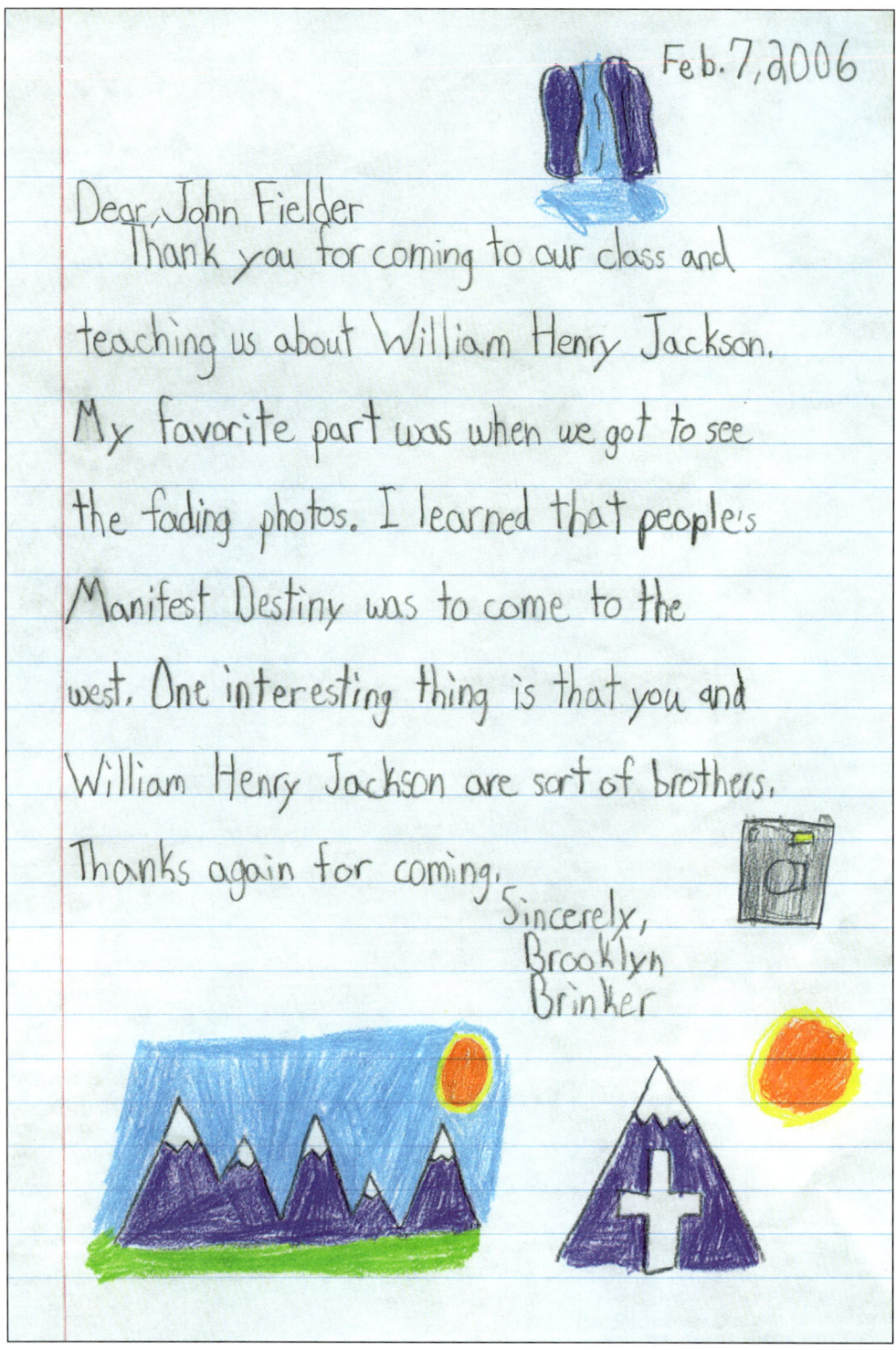

A letter from Brooklyn Brinker to John Fielder

Chapter Seven: John, the Photographer

The trail to the top of Longs Peak. The Boulder Field and Longs Peak, 1901, W.H. Jackson and John Fielder, 1998. In order to stand exactly where Jackson stood to take this picture, John had to find the same rocks in a field of millions of rocks! Do you see the same rocks?

again from the exact same place that Jackson stood, pointing his camera in the same direction. Three books with the common title *Colorado 1870-2000* were published. All three became Colorado's best-selling books of all time. People enjoyed comparing the changes in the landscape, which sometimes were great and sometimes very little. They noticed that some changes were for the better, others were not.

During the W. H. Jackson project, John returned to Longs Peak to replicate a photo. This time, contrary to his first visit in 1964, he did more than look up at the top. He hiked and climbed eight challenging miles to the summit. The trail went over and between large boulders, along narrow ledges, up a steep gully known as a "couloir", and finally, it scaled a sheer cliff to the top. John tenaciously tackled this carrying his 65-pound pack of photography equipment. He showed a lot of grit. John was not to be denied from taking this unique picture. Perseverance defines John's career and life.

This quotation explains John's passion for the outdoors: "Excellent photography reveals an emotional attach-

Carrying 65 pounds of camera gear to the top of Longs Peak!

Right: Comparing a W.H. Jackson photograph to John's instant Polaroid print in order to stand in the exact same location that Jackson stood over 100 years before

ment between a photographer and the subject matter. I hope people who view my images are impressed more by the integrity of nature than by the photography itself, and that my photography helps generate a greater appreciation for all things natural. I hope that people who see my work will visit natural places and understand nature in their own way." (*The Denver Post, Empire Magazine,* October 16, 1999.)

John's 7 Most Important Photo Tips for Photographers:

1. If you can't see it, you can't photograph it. Your eyes are what matter, not the quality of your camera. Use whatever you wish, cell phone to single lens reflex camera.

2. Half of good photography is being able to compose (arrange things in) a pretty picture, the other half is being in the right place at the right time. The more you go outdoors, the more you will be in the right place at the right time!

3. Photos are best during the "magic hours," one hour after sunrise and one hour before sunset. Shadows are broad and add depth to your scene, and the color of light is red, orange, or yellow.

4. In a beautiful place, or during pretty light, think about making three different pictures: a. the big view including landscape and sky, b. the small view, such as close-ups of

These mountains are really gray, but sunset makes them orange. Notice the shadows, too.

wildflowers, and c. the view in between those two: a picture with the landscape, but without the sky.

5. In order to create a scene that makes you feel like "you could lay out a picnic blanket and have a picnic," get really close to a beautiful thing, like wildflowers, and compose them in the bottom of the scene. Include the rest of the landscape, and sky if you wish, in the background. If you do this, the beautiful thing in the foreground will look bigger than it usually does compared to the background.

6. Leave No Trace is the name of an important organization, and it is also my personal ethic. Whether photographer or just visitor to nature, I hope you will allow others to follow in your footsteps as if you had not been there. My experience outdoors is always enhanced when I feel that I am the first person to ever be in a place. On-trail I know this is not true, but not seeing initials carved on trees or rocks stacked as cairn direction markers certainly helps. Never leave trash or toilet paper in nature, and take a small trowel bury your poop. When hiking off-trail, I step where no one else has stepped to minimize the chance of others following the same path. And as they say, "take" only pictures!

Do you like to take close-ups of Colorado columbine wildflowers as much as I do? This is our state flower.

Sumac berries in autumn, Raggeds Wilderness

CHAPTER 8

John
the Environmentalist

"A large part of my life is spent protecting and advocating for nature and biodiversity. Ansel Adams was my photographer hero because he was as much an environmentalist as he was a photographer," John said. "He used his photographs to promote advocacy of the protection of nature. I love photography, but I love nature more, and that influences my work." A protected habitat is the foundation for all species' survival, including plants, animals, and creatures in the water.

Conservation has been practiced for eons by Native Americans. They often used only what they needed from nature. Trees, animals, vegetation, and other items in nature were not wasted. Many of their spiritual practices were based on their reverence for the land, sky, water, and creatures that inhabit them. They saw themselves as being a part of nature but not in charge of it. Living in harmony with the world around them was a priority, as well as a way to survive.

> *With beauty before me, may I walk*
> *With beauty behind me, may I walk*
> *With beauty above me, may I walk,*
> *With beauty below me, may I walk*
> *With beauty all around me, may I walk*
> *Wandering on a trail of beauty, lively, I walk*
> Navajo Indians

Sunflowers, Great Sand Dunes National Park and Preserve

Humans are finally beginning to understand that the natural bounty of the land is not infinite, and that there is a price to pay for ignorance of those limits. Deforestation eliminates trees that produce oxygen and absorb carbon dioxide, a heat-trapping greenhouse gas. It is estimated that a single tree can absorb the carbon emissions of a car driven 26,000 miles. Three trees contribute enough oxygen for one person to breathe. Energy extraction and mineral mining have created many jobs. Most of our transportation and building materials are built with minerals. On the other hand, these industries have had a devastating impact on the natural environment. Oil drilling has spilled oil onto land and into oceans and poisoned the air. Mineral mining has released water laced with poisonous heavy metals into rivers and creeks, killing aquatic life for decades.

John walking with beauty all around him

Worse yet, the burning of fossil fuels has warmed Earth by sending an excess of carbon dioxide, CO_2, into the air. Coal burned in power plants and gasoline burned by automobiles emit most of the CO_2. This accelerates global warming by forming a shield over the Earth

Oil & gas extraction near the Pawnee Buttes, Pawnee National Grasslands

that absorbs solar radiation. Methane gas comes from livestock and industry. An ever-increasing amount of methane is produced by the death of life forms under warming oceans, from under melting ice sheets, and even from warming reservoirs around the globe. Methane absorbs heat from the sun 84 times more effectively than carbon dioxide. These are the major causes of the manmade greenhouse effect. This warms the Earth faster than natural causes.

The science of climate change is incontrovertible, as is the fact that we humans are causing it. The negative effects of global warming and climatic change cannot be underestimated. Higher temperatures result in a hotter and drier climate. High temperatures put stress on plants and animals, as well as human beings. The polar ice caps and Greenland ice sheet are melting faster than scientists ever imagined, causing ocean water levels to rise. Global warming is a threat to our economy and jobs, and the survival of humanity and biodiversity.

"The speed with which Earth is warming is alarming," John said. "The time to act on global warming is now. By 2050, it will be too late.

Our greatest responsibility to our children and grandchildren is to slow global warming." Science and technology today provide alternative energy sources necessary to slow the warming. Other methods of energy production include solar, wind, and geothermal. Solar and wind power has expanded immensely nationwide over the last 11 years. In 2018, solar and wind accounted for 8.9% of the U.S. energy production. In order to understand how effective it already is, in March 2017, wind and solar energy accounted for 24% of all electricity production in Colorado.

"I am excited about the possibility of slowing global warming! So many people from all countries embrace the science of climate change, and millions more come on board each year. New leaders around the planet who support advanced climate policies, such as taxes on carbon-producing facilities and companies, are being elected into office. In America, state after state is banning fossil fuels used for their electricity supply and committing to be 100% clean energy. Globally, students have access to science and technology as never before. Our salvation lies in brilliant and thoughtful young people leading us forward!"

These are dead lodgepole pine trees on John's property in Summit County. The pine bark beetles killed them and millions more on 3.5 million acres of land in Colorado in the past 25 years. Global warming prevents the cold temperatures that are necessary to kill these insects while they live in the bark of the trees during the winter. In the spring, the beetles reproduce and fly away to kill more trees.

Chapter Eight: John, the Environmentalist   91

John and his grandkids at home in Summit County

John Fielder has been an active leader for protecting nature in Colorado. In 1980, Colorado voters approved a state lottery to raise money to build more parks and buy open space (land to be preserved). Then the state legislature started using a large portion of the funds to build prisons and other buildings. In 1992, The Great Outdoors Colorado Trust Fund (GOCO) initiative was placed on the ballot. It proposed to spend all the lottery money to build parks and preserve open space. John traveled all over Colorado to talk passionately to communities about the initiative. Colorado voters showed they cared about preservation by approving the initiative. GOCO has spent more than $1.2 billion of lottery proceeds on 5,200 land protection projects, including creation or restoration of 900 miles of trails and 1,100 parks.

John and his family celebrate with Colorado Governor Roy Romer the passage of the GOCO initiative in 1992

John was appointed to the GOCO board of trustees by Governor Romer. He also published a picture book and guidebook about many of these places that benefited and promoted GOCO and its work (*John Fielder's Great Outdoors Colorado*, 2012).

In 1991, U.S. Senator Timothy Wirth from Colorado introduced a law in the United States Congress to add 750,000 acres in Colorado to the National Wilderness Preservation System. The law that made this possible is the Wilderness Act of 1964. Senator Wirth suspected that boundaries on maps might not be enough evidence to convince Congress to act. He asked John to take pictures of these areas. For the next year and a half, John voluntarily backpacked and used llamas to carry his gear throughout the 750,000 acres to take the photos. These pictures were published in a book,

The book that helped pass the Colorado Wilderness Act of 1993

Chapter Eight: John, the Environmentalist   93

Colorado, Our Wilderness Future. It was passed out to all members of Congress and sold to the public. The beautiful images in this book helped convince lawmakers to pass the Colorado Wilderness Act of 1993.

In 1993, John was invited to give an interview on the NBC nightly news about the Act. It was at Maroon Lake, near the Maroon Bells (14,000-foot) peaks. This was close to Aspen, Colorado and it occurred

The photograph that John took during the interview with NBC Nightly News

on a snowy December morning. The TV crew and John rode in snowmobiles up to the area. John set up his tripod and camera. Then, he turned and saw mist rising from the lake and snow blowing off the peaks. Not one to miss a perfect photo opportunity, John said, "Interview suspended." He quickly took a picture of the beautiful mountain scene. Then, the interview continued. That evening, the interview was shown on the NBC nightly news with Tom Brokaw.

As a result of the news interview, Senator Wirth invited John to project his wilderness photographs on a screen and talk to 500 people

John talking to the Plant Select nonprofit organization at Denver Botanic Gardens in June, 2019. John raised $1,000 for Plant Select from book sales that day.

about the new wilderness areas. This event was held at the University of Denver Law School. "It was the defining moment when I became an environmentalist," John recalled. "I always appreciated nature, but I wasn't an advocate publicly. I had not performed slide shows to large crowds, so that was a milestone." John's presentation was a huge success. Since then, he performs up to 40 slide shows each year in Colorado to thousands of people. He always shows his beautiful pictures with music in the background and tells his entertaining stories about his life on the trail.

In 2000, John used his growing visibility and experience with ballot initiatives to partner with the Colorado Environmental Coalition and Colorado Public Interest Research Group. Together, they put the Responsible Growth Initiative, Amendment 24, on the November ballot. Colorado had just seen its population grow from 3.3 to 4.2 million people from 1990 to 2000. Cheap farmland on the outskirts of Front Range cities was being converted into housing developments at an unprecedented rate. This "sprawl" was an uneconomical form of growth. This was due to the high cost of connecting communities to water and electric services. It also was expensive to finance fire, police, and road improvements. Open space was being destroyed at an alarming rate.

John speaking on the steps of the Colorado State Capitol to promote the passage of Amendment 24

John traveled all over Colorado to speak to dozens of communities. He passionately talked about the need to give local governments more control over managing the growth of towns and cities. Unfortunately, the real estate industry raised an unprecedented amount of money for an initiative campaign, about $7 million. It defeated Amendment 24 by painting it as a "no growth" plan. John said, "We simply wanted to make it easier for Coloradans to decide how, when, where, and why a community would grow. This would reduce the costs of growth and at the same time, protect Colorado's extraordinary ecosystems."

Water protection is one of John's priorities and passions. Its quality and quantity are adversely affected by global warming. Rivers are ecosystems for thousands of lifeforms, and they depend upon water that flows freely. John is on the board of directors of **SaveTheColorado.org**. and works with **SaveThePoudre.org**. These organizations work to prevent more water from being taken from the Colorado and Poudre Rivers. Both rivers have been extensively dammed and diverted, and there are plans for more of the same. Instead of taking more water from rivers, John would like people to conserve more water.

Eighty-five percent of the water in Colorado is used by agriculture. Farmers and ranchers do not use all their water every year. John suggests we buy this unused water to supply our needs. Agriculture is a $12 billion per year industry in Colorado. Oil and gas exploration and production produce about $25 billion in revenues. According to the U.S. Department of Labor, in 2018, the mining, logging, and oil and gas industries created 30,400 jobs. According to the Division of Colorado Parks & Wildlife, outdoor recreation brings in $62 billion a year and generates 511,000 jobs. "It is pretty obvious that protecting blue skies, clean air, clean water, free-flowing rivers, building more parks and trails on federal, state, and local lands (not undoing them, which happened to some National Monuments in 2016), and protecting our ranches from development is the best way to make money and jobs in Colorado," stated John.

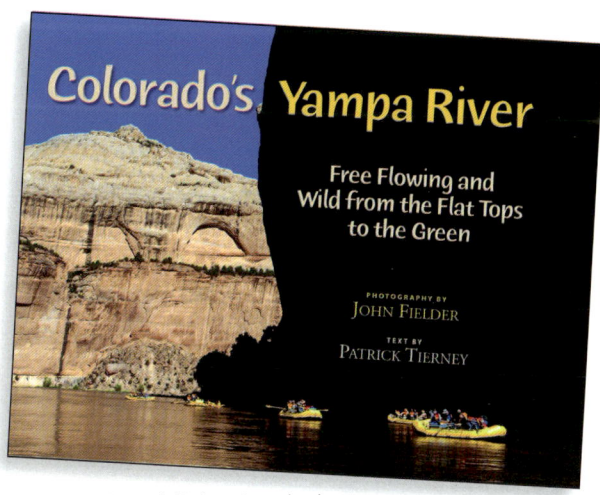

The book published to help to save the Yampa River in northwest Colorado

Like his father who contributed to his home community, John helps the community of people like him that loves the outdoors and nature. John has published books that raised money to finance environmental and conservation nonprofit organizations. For example, in 1992 and 1993, John hiked the 470-mile long Colorado Trail and took pictures for the Colorado Trail Foundation. The photos were put into a coffee table book, *Along the Colorado Trail,* and a companion guidebook to hiking the trail. Proceeds from both books benefited the foundation. John likes to publish books that encourage people to explore nature for themselves. "It is one thing to see pretty pictures of nature in a book, entirely another to smell it, taste it, touch it, and hear it, as well as see it," he explained. "Only if people have experienced firsthand the sensuousness of nature will they become advocates to vote to protect nature."

High country wildflowers along the Colorado Trail, Weminuche Wilderness

Chapter Eight: John, the Environmentalist

On the other hand, too many footprints in fragile natural places can do as much damage as energy extraction. It is a delicate balance. "We want more people to enjoy the benefits of nature. And it is also important to preserve the environment from overuse. We must invest more money at the federal, state, and local levels to

Some of John's other books have contributed to conservation efforts. Here are a few:

Rocky Mountain National Park, A 100 Year Perspective, 1995 – helped buy buffer land (free from housing or business development) around Rocky Mountain National Park for the Rocky Mountain Conservancy.

Along Colorado's Continental Divide Trail picture book and guidebook, 1997 – the construction and maintenance of the Continental Divide National Scenic Trail

Ranches of Colorado, 2009 – benefitted land trusts (organizations set up to protect land) and promoted protecting ranches from development with conservation easements (contracts set up to protect land)

Denver Mountain Parks: 100 Years of the Magnificent Dream, 2013 – raised funds and awareness to protect and maintain 14,000 acres in Denver's Mountain Parks

Nadia's Good Deed, 2014 – raised funds to build schools and water infrastructure (water pipes and pumps) in remote Haitian villages.

Colorado's Yampa River: Free Flowing and Wild Forever, 2015 – raised funds and awareness to keep the waters of the Yampa River undammed and never diverted to the Front Range

John and Rachel Harris, co-author of *Nadia's Good Deed*, promote the book on KWGN television in 2014

manage the very places we love and have set aside for human recreation. Why save it if we cannot protect it?"

John has a familiar pattern for using books for his environmental efforts. First, he takes photos of an area considered for preservation. Next, he uses these photos to make a book about saving this land. Then, he donates part or all of the book's profits to a nonprofit advocacy organization. About 90% of John's slide presentations are made for no fee to non-profit environmental and humanitarian organizations. At these presentations, he donates 30% of the book sales back to the sponsoring organization. Every year, John also donates many of his valuable fine art photographs and spaces in his popular—and usually

John shows his pictures on massive screens to accompany the music of live bands and orchestras. Here the John Adams Band and John perform a John Denver Tribute (that's a lot of Johns!) The event raised money for Domus Pacis, a Summit County nonprofit organization that provides relief to families who take care of family members with cancer.

Chapter Eight: John, the Environmentalist   101

Aboard the U.S.S. Colorado submarine

sold out—photography workshops. These are auctioned by environmental and humanitarian organizations at their annual fundraising events. Some people do not agree with John's pro-conservation efforts. They may not buy his books or calendars because of this difference of opinion. This does not deter John from helping those people and organizations in need.

In 2018, John donated many of his large-format Colorado panoramic photographs to the U.S. Navy. They are permanently mounted in the crew's quarters (where the crew sleeps and recreates) and mess area (cafeteria) of the U.S.S. Colorado. It is our newest Virginia Class nuclear attack submarine. These photographs improve the daily life on the sub for the 134 crew members when they are out on multi-month tours of duty. John was invited to the launch ceremonies of the submarine in Groton, Connecticut. He toured the 377-foot-long submarine and even got to drive the submarine simulator that trains the crew that operates the sub. During the simulation he claims, "I crashed the sub trying to steer it too vertically to the surface of the ocean!"

Recently, John showed new pictures at the Colorado History Center. The audience saw images from John's 2018 book, *Colorado Black on White*. The pictures were so lifelike that in the darkened room, the audience felt like they were actually with John in the natural settings. John passionately talked about the impacts of oil and gas extraction, preservation of water, and the effects of global warming. As usual, 30% of the book sales were donated to the museum. In fact, the total sales of books in the *Colorado 1870-2000* series have generated $500,000 for the museum.

Discussing the value of wilderness in Colorado

Chapter Eight: John, the Environmentalist 103

John Fielder, the environmentalist, by Madison Leinster, 5th grade

John enjoys visiting schools and showing his photographs to the students. He talks to children of all ages about his profession and life, including Mrs. Hickman's influence on him at their age, and how their lives might be changed by their own teachers. The students love seeing pictures of John's children in the outdoors when they were young, and especially enjoy the photographs of, and stories about, the llamas.

John's most significant achievements in life have not been starting a successful publishing business from scratch or becoming the foremost

John talking to the students of Meadow View Elementary School in Castle Rock, Colorado

Whitey, the Flying Llama

"In 2002, I spent a week in the West Elk Wilderness near Crested Butte, Colorado. On the first night, my three human companions and I camped on top of Storm Pass at 12,496 feet above sea level. It was the first week of July, and there was a lot of snow still covering the north side of the mountain. The next morning, we discovered that the trail descending to the next valley was entirely covered by snow all the way to the bottom. We decided to test if the llamas could glissade (slide down) on the snow. I unhooked the one named Whitey from the other two and led him to the edge of the steep part of the mountain. His front legs soon 'post-holed' (sunk) in the soft snow all the way up to his chest. He lost his balance, began plunging downhill, and then did three complete full-frontal body flips in mid-air before landing on his back. He continued to slide down the mountain on the snow backward and upside-down at 40 miles per hour."

"I looked over at the other people, and they all had their mouths wide open in disbelief. Then I looked over at the other two llamas, and they had their mouths wide open, too! I had never seen llamas look like this. Whitey came to a complete stop 800 vertical feet below us, just before the snow ended and the big rocks began. From far away I could see him stand up. Apparently, he was OK. I asked the guys to take the llamas down the mountain a different way where the snow had melted, and I glissaded down to Whitey. He was shaking, but unharmed. Whitey completed the trip six days later with the rest of us."

Whitey, the flying llama, surveying the snow from Storm Pass before trying to fly; and descending the bottom of Storm Pass after getting the three llamas back together again! Notice the "Castles," eroded volcanic ash formations, in the background.

nature photographer in Colorado. His greatest accomplishment has been raising environmental awareness to the public. John promotes the necessity of doing all we can to protect nature and biodiversity in Colorado and beyond. His legacy will be the part he played in giving humanity a chance to avoid extinction.

Pope Francis receives a copy of John's book *Mountain Ranges of Colorado* at the Vatican in Rome, Italy in 2018. A Denver doctor's brother is a priest at the Vatican, and he arranged an audience for his family with the Pope. John's books are used as gifts around the world to celebrate the extraordinary beauty of Colorado.

The beauty of the trees, the softness of the air,
the fragrance of the grass... speaks to me.
The summit of the mountain, the thunder of the sky
the rhythm of the sea... speaks to me.
The faintness of the stars, the freshness of the morning
the dewdrop on the flower... speaks to me.
The strength of fire, the taste of salmon, the trail of the sun
and the life that never goes away.
They speak to me and my heart soars
—Dan George
(Chief of Tsleil-Waututh Nation) 1899 – 1981

Cascade, Rocky Mountain National Park

Epilogue

Twenty-five years after his second summer traveling with Mrs. Hickman, John had by then published four books. He had lost touch with her, but not forgotten her. He mailed copies of these books to her with a note, "You are the reason why these books exist." John was acknowledging Mrs. Hickman's influence on his life. Every year thereafter, until her death at age 96 in 2014, John visited her in North Carolina. Either they would take a drive into the Blue Ridge Mountains, during which she would recite the names of every visible wildflower (including common and Latin names!), or just have lunch and talk about old times. Every year, she would say to John: "I remember when you told me in Rocky Mountain National Park in the summer of 1964 that you would live in Colorado someday."

I dedicate this book to the memory of
Mrs. Eunice "Dolly" Hickman
July 17, 1918 – November 9, 2014

This is an image of a single columbine wildflower growing from a crack in a rock in Colorado's Weminuche Wilderness. It was reproduced into prints and posters in 1999, shortly after the tragedy at Columbine High School, April 20. With the help of the Littleton Rotary Club, the sales raised $150,000, which was used to help those who were injured at Columbine with their medical expenses.

Selected Accomplishments and Awards

Daniel L. Ritchie Award for Ethical Behavior and Social Responsibility (University of Denver, 1992)

Colorado Conservation Award (Colorado Chapter of the Nature Conservancy, 1992)

Ansel Adams Award for Conservation Photography (Sierra Club, 1993)

Rocky Mountain National Park Stewardship Award (Rocky Mountain National Park, 1995)

Cranmer Award (Colorado Open Lands, 1997)

Humanitarian Award (National Recreation and Parks Association, 1998)

John receiving his honorary degree

Distinguished Service Award (University of Colorado, 2000)

Rebel with a Cause (Colorado Environmental Coalition, 2007)

Lifetime Achievement Award (Colorado Film Commission, 2007)

Aldo Leopold Foundation (first ever Achievement Award to an individual by that organization, 2011)

Colorado Mountain College Honorary Degree Sustainability Studies, 2017

Locoweed wildflowers below Pawnee Buttes, Pawnee National Grasslands

Timeline

1950: John is born in Washington, D.C.

1952: Fielder family moves to Rye, New York

1956: John Fielder, Sr. starts new job, family moves to Greenwich, Connecticut

1960: John Sr. and family move to Charlotte, North Carolina after starting a new job

John begins attending Charlotte Country Day School

1960-63: John goes to Camp Sequoyah summer camp

1960: John begins taking photos with the Brownie Box camera

1963-64: cross-country field trips with Mrs. Dolly Hickman

1967: ranch hand at Naja Ranch near Westcliffe, Colorado

1967-68: art classes with Mr. Birch

1968: John works at John Sr.'s department store

John begins college at Duke University

1969-70: John works as junior geologist in Colorado and nearby states for Uncle Fred

1971: John works in John Sr.'s department store

1972: John graduates from Duke University and moves to Colorado

1972-73: John works in real estate

1973: department store career begins

John rents a Pentax camera

John buys a Canon camera

1975: John meets Virginia "Gigi" Yonkers

1977: John starts using a 4" x 5" large format camera

1978: John and Gigi get married

1980: Son JT is born

1981: John leaves department store work to begin his career in photography

John publishes first Colorado calendar

1982: Daughter Ashley is born

John starts Westcliffe Publishers

John publishes first book *Colorado's Hidden Valleys*

1985: Daughter Katy is born

1992-93: John works on Colorado Wilderness Act project and speaks for the first time to an audience about environmental issues

1992: John travels extensively around Colorado to talk about GOCO

1998: Gigi's early onset Alzheimer's disease is discovered

1999: John Fielder/W.H. Jackson's *Colorado 1870-2000* is published

2004: John Fielder Sr. passes away

2005: Gigi passes away from Alzheimer's disease

2006: JT takes his own life

2007: John sells Westcliffe Publishers

John moves to Summit County

2009: John's mother, Betsy Fielder passes away

2009: John starts John Fielder Publishing

John and Tommie, the llama

Glossary

accounting: keeping a record of business money and how to use it wisely

adversity: hardship

advocate: a person who speaks or writes in support or defense of a cause

Alzheimer's disease : Alzheimer's disease is an irreversible, progressive brain disorder that slowly destroys memory and thinking skills and, eventually, the ability to carry out the simplest tasks. (National Institute of Health)

auspicious: promising future success

backcountry skiing: skiing in mountainous areas outside of commercial ski resorts

ballot: a method by which people vote

board: group of people that make decisions

carbon emissions: carbon dioxide produced from burning fossil fuels

consternation: dismay

constrained: restricted

coveted: most desired

cross-country skiing: skating across the land on narrow skis

early onset: beginning at an early age

elicited: drew out

embedded: implanted

enhanced: improved or increased

entrepreneurial: taking financial risk with the hope of profit

escarpment: a long, steep slope

extraction: pulling something out by force

four-wheel-drive: power from the engine is delivered to all 4 wheels

geochemical: chemical composition of minerals in the Earth

hypothermia: abnormally low body temperature

incontrovertible: not open to question or dispute

indelibly: that cannot be eliminated, forgotten, or changed

initiative: law created by the public, not by the state legislature

investor: the person who puts money into a deal expecting profits

lobbied: influenced

lore: stories

lottery: a method of raising money in which a large number of tickets are sold, and a drawing is held for certain prizes

merchandising: selling

military draft lottery: the military assigned numbers to men's birthdates, then randomly picked the numbers to see who would be required to serve in the military

molybdenum: mineral used to harden and strengthen steel

nonprofit: uses money earned for a social cause – like conservation

politics: use of ways in obtaining any position of power or control, as in business

precipitous: steep

processed film: film is processed into negatives or transparencies which are made into pictures.

remains: a dead body; corpse

sensuous: perceived by or affecting the senses

sentient: having the power of perception by the senses; conscious

stamp mill: where ore is crushed to dust using a heavy "stamp" (hammer)

stigmatized: marked by disgrace

survey: closely examine

Thoreau: 19th-century naturalist and philosopher

topographical: how the mountains, plains, rivers, fields, streams, valleys or hills are arranged

unprecedented: never before known or experienced

35mm camera: camera which takes pictures recorded on a roll of film, which was then processed into photos

4x5 camera: these take 4x5 inch images that can be enlarged into huge crystal-clear pictures

Bibliography

Anderson, Peter. *Aldo Leopold American Ecologist.* Danbury, Connecticut: Franklin Watts, 1995

Anderson, Peter. *John Muir: Wilderness Prophet.* Danbury, Connecticut: Franklin Watts, 1995

Anderson, Peter. *Henry David Thoreau Naturalist.* Danbury, Connecticut: Franklin Watts, 1995

Arato, Rona. *World of Water Essential to Life.* New York, New York: Crabtree Publishing, 2005

Campbell, Sarah. *Mysterious Patterns Finding Fractals in Nature.* Honesdale, Pennsylvania: Boyds Mills Press, 2014

Carson, Rachel. *The Sense of Wonder.* New York and Evanston: Harper and Row, 1956

Cherry, Lynne. *The Great Kapok Tree.* New York: Harcourt, 1990

Cornell, Joseph. *John Muir My Life with Nature.* Nevada City, California: Dawn Publications, 2000

Dowd, John. *Ring of Tall Trees.* Bothel, Washington: Alaska Northwest Books, 1992

Dr. Suess. *The Lorax.* New York: Random House, 1971

Dunlap, Julie. *Eye on the Wild.* Minneapolis: Carolrhoda Books, 1995

Foss, Phillip (Editor). *Colorado and the Environment A Handbook.* Ft. Collins, Colorado Environmental Resource Center, Colorado State University, 1973.

Hand, Carol. *Women in Conservation Women in STEM.* Minneapolis, Minnesota: Abdo Publishing, 2017

Hand, Carol. *Coral Reef Collapse.* Minneapolis, Minnesota: 2018

Harris, Rachel. *Nadia's Good Deed.* Silverthorne, Colorado: John Fielder Publishing, 2014

Hicks, Dwayne. *Solving the Energy Crisis.* New York, New York: Rosen Publishing, 2017

Iyer, Rani. *Endangered Energy Investigating the Scarcity of Fossil Fuels.* North Mankato, Minnesota: Capstone Press, 2015120

Iyer, Rani. *Endangered Rivers Investigating Rivers in Crisis.* North Mankato, Minnesota: Capstone Press, 2015

Jankowski, Matt. *Be a Conservationist!* New York, New York: Gareth Stevens Publishing, 2019

Labrecque, Elle. *Clean Water Global Citizens: Environmentalism.* Ann Arbor, Michigan: Cherry Lake, 2018

Lasky, Kathryn. *John Muir America's First Environmentalist.* Cambridge, Massachusetts: Candlewick Press, 2006

Levy, Jani. *Inside the Environmental Movement Clean Air Inside Out.* New York, New York: Gareth Stevens Publishing, 2018

Locker, Thomas and Bruchac, Joseph. *Rachel Carson Preserving a Sense of Wonder.* Golden, Colorado: Fulcrum, 2004

Love, Ann and Drake, Jane. *Take Action World Wildlife Fund.* New York: Tamborine Books, 1993

Marsico, Katie. *How Do They Help? The Nature Conservancy.* Ann Arbor, Michigan: Cherry Lake Publishing, 2017

McAdam, Claudia Cangilla. *Do You See What I See?* Englewood, Colorado: Westcliffe Publishers, 2006

McAdam, Claudia Cangilla. *A, B, See Colorado An Alphabet book of the Centennial State.* Silverthorne, Colorado: John Fielder Publishing, 2012

McAdam, Claudia Cangilla. *Maria's Mysterious Mission.* Boulder, Colorado: Westcliffe Publishers, 2007

McCarthy, Michael G. *Hour of Trial The Conservation Conflict in the West, 1891-1907.* Norman, Oklahoma: University of Oklahoma Press, 1977

Mooney, Carl. *Rivers and Ponds!* White River Junction, Vermont: Nomad Press, 2012

Mulder, Michelle. *Going Wild Helping Nature Thrive in Cities.* Canada: Orca Book Publishers, 2018

Silverstein, Shel. *The Giving Tree.* New York, New York: Harper Collins Publishers, 1964

Vale, Thomas R. *The American Wilderness.* Rector and Visitors of the University of Virginia: University of Virginia Press, 2005

Walsh, Steve. *Enos Mills Rocky Mountain Conservationist.* Palmer Lake, Colorado: Filter Press, 2011

Waterman, Laura and Guy. *Wilderness Ethics Preserving the Spirit of Wildness.* Woodstock, Vermont: The Countryman Press, 1993

John's Selected Conservation Organizations

Audubon – www.audobon.org
Colorado Cattlemen's Agricultural Land Trust – www.ccalt.org
Colorado Open Lands – www.coloradoopenlands.org
Conservation Colorado – www.conservationco.org
Conservation International – www.conservation.org
Defenders of Wildlife – www.defenders.org
Earth Justice – www.earthjustice.org
Environment Colorado – www.environmentcolorado.org
Great Outdoors Colorado (GOCO) – www.goco.org
High Country Conservation Advocates – www.hccacb.org
League of Conservation Voters – www.lcv.org
National Parks Conservation Association – www.npca.org
National Parks Foundation – www.nationalparks.org
National Resources Defense Council – www.nrdc.org
National Wildlife Federation – www.nwf.org
Nature Conservancy – www.nature.org
Oceana – https.oceana.org
Rocky Mountain Climate Organization – www.rockymountainclimate.org
Rocky Mountain Conservancy – www.rmconservancy.org
Save the Colorado – www.savethecolorado.org
Save the Poudre – www.savethepoudre.org
Sierra Club – www.sierraclub.org
Trust for Public Lands – www.tpl.org
Western Resource Advocates – www.westernresourceadvocates.org
Wild Earth Guardians – www.wildearthguardians.org
Wilderness Workshop – www.wildernessworkshop.org
Wilderness Land Trust – www.wildernesslandtrust.org
Wilderness Society, The – www.wilderness.org
Wildlife Society – www.wildlife.org
Wildlife Conservation Society (WCS) – www.wcs.org
World Wildlife Fund – www.worldwildlife.org

Steve Walsh

This book is dedicated to Cara and Oliver, my grandchildren, whose sense of wonder, curiosity, and appreciation of nature make any and all efforts for conservation worthwhile.

A large debt of gratitude goes to John Fielder, who's generosity and extra effort has made this book possible. I have been impressed by his deep appreciation of family, friends, and nature. John's undefeatable drive for the preservation of Colorado's landscape benefits us all. I am also grateful to Sue Lubeck, owner of The Bookies Bookstore, who has championed children's appreciation of books and has been a great advocate for teachers. I appreciate Miriam, my wife, whose ongoing support greatly encourages my work as a writer. She has contributed many ideas towards this biography, which helped bring John's story to life.

Steve Walsh grew up in Wayland, Massachusetts and loved spending time in the woods, fields, and ponds near his home. These early encounters with nature led to him to enjoy outdoor experiences in California, Colorado, and other Western States. Steve, a former counselor and elementary school teacher, and Miriam, have lived in Denver over forty years. Together, they raised four children: Shannon, Peggy, Katie, and Brian. Wanting to make Colorado history accessible to young readers, Steve has written five other published biographies: Enos Mills, Zebulon Pike, Chief Ouray, Bill Hosokawa, and Stephen H. Long.

Sunrise on Mount Yale, Collegiate Peaks Wilderness

ISBN: 978-0-9985080-8-5
TEXT COPYRIGHT: Steve Walsh 2019. All Rights Reserved
PHOTOGRAPHY COPYRIGHT: John Fielder 2019. All Rights Reserved
PUBLISHED BY: John Fielder Publishing
POB 26890 | Silverthorne, Colorado 80497
GRAPHIC DESIGN: Rebecca Finkel, F + P Graphic Design
EDITOR: Claudia Cangilla McAdam

PRINTED IN CANADA

No portion of this book, either text or photographs, may be reproduced in any form without the express written consent of the publisher.

Quantity book sales: visit www.JohnFielder.com
Book resellers contact Caleb Seeling: caleb@ImprintGroupWest.com

Invite John to Your School!
John enjoys talking to students of all ages and showing his pictures on the slide screen. April, May, the first half of September, the last half of October, November, and December are the best times for him to visit. Contact John directly john@johnfielder.com

John Fielder Slide Shows
John enjoys taking a break from the "trail" in order to perform public and private multi-media shows, live music collaborations, and book signings. Come to an event or invite him to present to your organization.

John Fielder Photography Workshops
John enjoys sharing his knowledge of photography with others. This is your opportunity to learn nature photography directly from John in Colorado's most scenic locales, and, from time to time, in other states and countries.

John Fielder Fine Art Prints
John provides many ways to graphically bring his nature photographs, both color and black and white, into homes, offices, institutions, and public places. He has 1,000 images online. For images from this book, refer to page numbers.

For complete information visit **www.JohnFielder.com**
To contact John: **john@johnfielder.com**

Conservation Websites for Kids

https://easyscienceforkids.com/all-about-conservation/

https://learn.eartheasy.com/articles/environmental-websites-for-kids/

https://www.biologicaldiversity.org/youth/conservation_for_kids.html

https://www.ducksters.com/animals/wildlife_conservation.php

https://www.kidsdiscover.com/shop/issues/conservation-for-kids/

Videos

Ansel Adams – *The American Experience,* Public Broadcasting Service, Steeplechase Films, 2002

Carson, Rachel – *A sense of wonder: two interviews based on the life and writings of Rachel Carson,* Public Broadcasting Service, Sense of Wonder Productions, 2010

Nye, Bill. *Way Cool Game of Science Population and Ecosystems.* Disney Education Productions.

School House Rock. Walt Disney Studio Science Kids

All About Energy. Wonderscope Entertainment

We love you JT